CALLED OUT

KELLEN ROGGENBUCK

CALLED OUT

Discerning God's Plan for Your Church

Abingdon Press
Nashville

CALLED OUT:
DISCERNING GOD'S PLAN FOR YOUR CHURCH

Copyright © 2025 by Abingdon Press

ISBN: 9781791037031

Library of Congress Control Number has been requested.

MANUFACTURED IN THE UNITED STATES OF AMERICA

Contents

Contents

Preface

A few things happened to bring this book into existence. First, in the fall of 2021, I was asked to be part of a teaching team for the Iowa United Methodist Church Licensing School teaching Evangelism and Discipleship. The Iowa Annual Conference had been developing, documenting, and implementing discipleship pathways, so this was an obvious focus for the licensing school. Soon-to-be pastors were getting a weeklong crash course about everything they'd need to begin leading the churches where they were appointed. My teaching partner and I explained what a discipleship pathway was, how to identify the gaps in the current church's ministry offerings, and how to discern new ministry and discipleship offerings to cover those gaps.

Teaching discipleship through the lens of discerning new faith expressions alongside discussions of personal, pastoral, and institutional evangelism had two main consequences: First, the students got to experience both evangelism and discipleship woven together through the call and creativity of new faith expressions, which inspired them to begin a journey of discernment to discover what the Holy Spirit was up to in their church's midst. Second, it inspired me to delve more deeply into the concept of discerning new faith expressions, church innovations, and pushing beyond the boundaries of what the local church in my own setting had ever done.

In the spring of 2023, I attended a day-and-a-half workshop on discernment provided as part of a series of teachings through the Wisconsin United Methodist Church focused on congregational development, especially new faith expressions and church planting. The description of this lecture seemed like exactly what I had been spending my free time researching and obsessing over. I showed up early, got a good seat, silenced my cell phone, and was ready to have my mind blown. Unfortunately, I found that the bulk of the teaching in that workshop described the need for discerning new faith expressions through inspiring but ancient biblical texts such as the Great Commission (Matthew 28:16-20) and specific examples of new faith expressions the speaker had implemented in his own ministry over the past several decades. Neither of these things are bad things for him to have done; I think that we should be able to bring scripture into discussions of discernment.

Likewise, I believe that sharing the innovations and new expressions that have succeeded within our own contexts is a powerful way to inspire others to begin the discernment process and may even provide an idea with which to start. The Great Commission is a wonderful place to start talking about the call to meeting people in new places. The issue in this particular workshop was that pastors were coming together desperately hoping for guidance in a post-lockdown, post-pandemic space in the midst of a denominational fracturing. In the end, it felt like a paramedic explaining to car crash victims that the road they were on was very dangerous, then describing the safer roads nearby instead of helping the victims into the ambulance and driving them to a hospital.

The need for new faith expressions is more profoundly realized in this modern season than any in the last few decades. Generation Z is both the largest generation ever and the least churched. We are now decades into a "post-Christian world." The COVID-19 pandemic was a brutal time for churches, and many did not reopen their doors. Our beloved Church is quickly becoming a series of beautiful empty buildings.

So what does that mean for the Church?
For your church?
For you as a church leader?
For you as a disciple of Jesus Christ?

In the process of completing this book, I had the opportunity to sit down with Michael Beck, Director of the Fresh Expressions House of Studies and adjunct professor at United Theological Seminary, to discuss the church's opportunity to follow God into exciting new spaces. We agreed that the long and rich heritage of innovation in the church is as much a part of our future as it has been our past. Beck has the opportunity to travel the country witnessing and consulting in spaces where the church is venturing into uncharted territories while embodying a timeless spirit of innovation. He shared with me his own excitement seeing God move and the church follow.

That is the dance of discernment; God takes the lead, and the church is invited to faithfully follow. When it is done well, the world opens before us and we get a glimpse of the coming kingdom of God.

I hope this book can help light a spark in you; that it can be just the beginning of a new relationship—a partnership—with the Holy Spirit who is already at work in your community. My hope is that the spark can spread, becoming a flame in you, in your leadership, in your church, until it is a blaze of creativity, hope, and unapologetic departure from the norm. The church grew from a band of first-century Jewish peasants meeting by candlelight in secret to mega-churches telecasting services over the internet to reach Christians around the globe. That growth happened through thousands (millions?) of innovations and cultural shifts. The Church did not just endure; it thrived. But in the US it seems the pinnacle has been reached and passed. And now, for many churches in our midst, it has become a time of fear, survival, struggle, and defeat. But there is still hope. Possibly more hope than ever before.

Now is a season of shift.

Now is an opportunity of innovation.

We are being called out of the past and into a season of newness.

We can endure and even thrive if we are brave enough to follow where God is desperately calling us to go.

Post-Christendom has brought new challenges. The Church's well-being is inextricably linked to how it seeks the well-being of the world around it. Inherited, attractional-only forms of church are not connecting with most people. We now need a blended ecology of church to thrive on a new missional frontier.

—Michael Beck, *New People // New Way*

The Point of Application

This resource accompanies *Called Out* as a tool to help you implement what you learn in the book. It provides a Point of Application for each chapter of the book. "Point of application" is a science term used when describing the specific location or point where a force is applied to an object. For our purposes, The Point of Application is when we use the knowledge gained through research and reading to create a product or establish a practice that makes an impact on our lives. The Point of Application process is designed as a group endeavor, for you to do with a team from your congregation. You can certainly work through the questions and activities alone, but the process will be more thorough and fruitful if done with leaders from your congregation. Each chapter's Point of Application offers specific questions or exercises to help you and your leadership teams work toward applying the knowledge gained in this book toward faithful and fruitful discernment.

Whenever we approach a book or a process of collaboration, we carry with us a set of questions and expectations. This book is a collaboration between me (the author), you, and the people in your leadership group. Before you begin reading this book, it may be helpful to outline your questions and expectations. Below are some questions to help you and your team develop a lens through which to read the book. You will find The Point of Application: An Implementation Resource for Congregational Leaders at abingdonpress.com/called-out-extras.

How would you describe your congregation today versus five years ago?
How would you describe the community in which the church serves today versus five years ago?
What questions are you hoping to have answered for you in the coming chapters?

Chapter 1

New Expressions

The sky is a glassy blue in the cloudless sky that afternoon, a gentle but persistent breeze coming in from the water. The shoreline is smattered with people—women washing their clothes in the shallows, children running and laughing and throwing rocks into the water. And there are even a few boats of fishermen having little luck catching anything but a sunburn. Some of them had given up, parking their boats on the shore and coming in to chat with those other people gathered at the beach. The soft murmur of talking and laughing are on the wind as it ripples the water, mingling the smell of the water with warm grass. It is a pleasant day like a hundred others on this shoreline on the Lake of Gennesaret in the first century. Then Jesus shows up.

Jesus shows up and the beach goers begin to notice him. Probably just one or two at first, but slowly word spreads from group to group who's here. People begin to press in to hear what's going on, hoping to catch a word or two. This is hardly surprising; Jesus is a bit of a local celebrity right now in Luke's Gospel. He's traveled a bit and done a few things, and it was likely the people gathered had at least heard his name before. He and his followers arrive at the lake and, as the crowd begins to form, Jesus doesn't disappoint; he begins with something amazing. There are several boats nearby on the shore and Jesus gets into one—Simon's boat—and asks Simon to let the boat drift out into the water a little bit. Once they had floated a little way, Jesus did this amazing thing, right there on the Lake of Gennesaret. He sat down right there in the boat and began to give a sermon.

At the time of Jesus, it was Jewish custom in the synagogue or temple to stand to read the scripture, then to sit and preach. Luke uses the language Jesus "sat down and taught" in the boat to indicate he is giving a sermon in the same way he would if he were in the local synagogue.

Right here, in Simon's boat, we witness a miracle. This day, on the lakeside, Jesus miraculously turned a beach into a holy temple. He brought the sacred space of the synagogue to the people gathered in this otherwise ordinary place, to the people who were likely in various stages of being ritually unclean and not welcome in the temple. All of a sudden, these people were on holy ground in the presence of the Almighty listening to the word of God. Jesus gave a sermon among the women washing their clothes and the children splashing while fishermen grumbled about their poor catch that morning, and a new faith expression was born.

Jesus created a new space for worship at the lakeside that day. A space without the pomp and circumstance of the holy temple, without gold-threaded paraments or religious art, without the grandeur and ostentatiousness of the temple itself, and without religious hierarchy. Instead, the message was equal for all who would listen. The wet clothes being washed were the paraments and all of creation was his holy sanctuary. Jesus made something new by bringing holy space to the people who needed it. It was outrageous for him to do so; the people gathered were exactly the type of people who weren't allowed into the temple because of their various afflictions or state of uncleanliness. It was completely out of line for Jesus to sidestep the religious orders of the time to transform this seaside into a holy space with all those people present.

He did it anyway.

In fact, that's why he did it.

New faith expressions are any ministry, worship, or outreach that meets people in a new way. In some cases, it is "New to You," something you haven't done before. In other cases, it's innovative or creative or borrowed from a non-church space and adapted to express a mission, outreach, or fellowship. In the best of cases, it's both.

Even two thousand years ago, Jesus was exploring new faith expressions, as in this story. He went to where the people were, specifically people who were disconnected from the local synagogue or temple, and with him he brought the good news of the gospel. This was a revolutionary act at the time.

God is calling us to try new things in new ways, to meet and serve new people. There's a common saying that "If you keep doing exactly what you are doing, you will continue to get the same results." We can easily get stuck in what we're currently doing, or what we used to do, and lament how it isn't bringing new people into discipleship. Coming out of COVID-19, looking at the dwindling attendance and diminishing budgets, it is easy to sink even further into an inward-focused institutional depression. But Jesus was preparing us for this from that lakeside millennia ago! He was showing how we can reach people in the world when we break free from our established comfort and go out into the world. When we follow Jesus's call into the world, we will find that there is new life and new hope within our churches and ministries.

Jesus is calling us to the lakesides, to the cafes and the bars.

Jesus is calling us to prisons and hospitals, libraries and schools.

Jesus is calling us supermarkets and salons, hardware stores and malls.

Jesus is even calling us to the internet, on new apps and in new media!

Jesus is calling us to the people, wherever they may be and in whatever state we may find them. New faith expressions are part of our institutional legacy, and it is time to focus on how we will adapt and grow into new spaces in this new age. Something new is needed. Whether it's simply new to your church or a brand-new expression. It may seem simple, but it is not without challenges. There is discernment to be done by pastors, congregations, and ministries to see where God is calling us to go. But make no mistake, Jesus is at work within your community, in a place your church is not, and is calling you out into that space among those people, inviting you to be a part of what is happening there.

How is it that we can respond to that call?

I am about to do a new thing;
now it springs forth; do you not perceive it?

—Isaiah 43:19a NRSVue

Chapter 2

Discernment and Calling

Called

A young man named Samuel lay in bed, awake. He was winding down from a long day of tending to the tabernacle. Nights were hard for Samuel sometimes, lying awake in the tabernacle thinking about the day. Sometimes he wondered what his mother was doing, what it would've been like to grow up like the other boys instead of sleeping just a few feet away from the covenant chest in this holy place. While other boys laid down to sleep in rooms with their siblings, their belongings strewn around with a general, comforting lived-in chaos, Samuel's room was only his—his and God's, that is. On other nights he was tired enough to fall asleep right away, but not tonight. Whether it was the wanderings in his mind, the unusual warmth of the evening, or something else, he wasn't quite ready to close his eyes.

"Samuel!" a voice called to him. It startled him in the darkness, in that vast space. It was a strong voice, with the authority and depth that usually was only present in the voice of Eli, Samuel's mentor. Eli called out to Samuel in the night sometimes.

5

His eyes had begun to fail him and he often needed help, though he didn't like to admit it. This must have been one of those nights, Samuel had thought, because there wasn't anyone else there.

The boy went to his master, quickly though reluctantly. "Here I am!" he announced. It was Eli's turn to be startled.

"What? Why are you here?" Eli questioned. Samuel looked at him, puzzled.

"You called me," he said slowly, wondering if perhaps Eli's memory was beginning to dim as his eyes had.

"Go back to bed. I didn't call you!" Eli said as he waived one hand, a hint of irritation in his tone, and so Samuel did. It wasn't like Eli to be so gruff to Samuel, but it was late, and Samuel was sure that Eli was as tired as he was. But as Samuel lay down again, he had hardly gotten comfortable when the voice called out to him again, "Samuel!" It was stronger, more insistent, though still from what felt like over some distance. The voice wasn't annoyed or stern, but knowing that Eli was already in bed and likely in need, Samuel ran again to Eli's room.

"Eli! I am here!" Samuel said, again entering the old man's room. Eli, who had also only just gotten comfortable and was growing less and less excited about interruption, sighed heavily and, though he could hardly make him out, stared hard in the direction Samuel was probably standing.

"What now, boy? I am tired and I bid that you only come to me when I call."

Samuel, again confused but reluctant to press the old man in this tired state again, left to return to bed. This was not how he wanted his night to end. Entering the tabernacle again, walking through the reverent silence that hung in the holy space, Samuel lain down once again. Why would Eli call, then not remember?

Clearly, it was his voice. There was no one else here. *Not unless God was talking to him*, Samuel thought, chuckling to himself. Though he was in the tabernacle, the holy place of God, God speaking to people was very rare. And even if it weren't, who was he that God would speak to him? The idea was absurd enough that he chuckled again as he laid his head down and closed his eyes, a smile on his face.

"Samuel!"

Samuel's eyes shot open; his smile was gone. The deep voice was clear now, and Samuel had expected to see Eli standing over him. But again, Samuel was alone, wondering if he dared go to Eli a third time. Even as he rose and ran to Eli's room, he prepared himself for a scolding. But the scolding would not come because as Samuel ran into Eli's room a third time, the old man didn't start or shout. He simply looked wearily toward the boy.

"I am here, master. I have heard a call three times now, what is it you require of me?" Samuel said quickly but strongly, hoping that this might jog the memory of the master. Eli did not answer immediately, but his face slowly shifted from the extreme tired he was feeling to one of something different—was it excitement? His cheeks seemed to grow rosy and though his eyes hadn't seemed to see Samuel that evening, a glint was present for just a flash.

"Boy," Eli said finally, "It is not I who calls you, but the Lord. No . . . listen," he said sternly, as Samuel began to interrupt, "go lie back down again, and if the voice returns, tell God that you are listening."

With that, Eli made a two-handed shooing motion. The hints of a smirk on his old face made it seem much younger. Samuel was not convinced, but in the years of service he had learned to trust the old man. So once more he headed through the tabernacle to lie down, not to sleep but to listen. Samuel grew still, concentrating on each sound around him, though the tent contained a heavy silence. After a moment, he realized that he was holding his breath. He let it out heavily, relaxing his body and drawing another deep breath. In the other room, as Eli lay in his bed in the darkness, he couldn't sleep, imagining what God might whisper in the dark to Samuel. Eli was a man of old faith, more than willing to have a conversation with God. But it was the young boy, calming his breathing, lying alone in that vast tent, trembling with anticipation that again heard the words, "Samuel! Samuel!"

Being ready for them had almost been more startling than having been roused from near sleep! Samuel took a sharp breath, sputtering out, "Yes Lord! I'm . . . I'm here! Your servant is listening!"

Your servant is listening.

In the stillness, in the trepidation, God was calling Samuel, and his response was listening.

This is God's calling.

That night God had told Samuel that something was coming and that Samuel's job was to tell Eli all about it. It was a simple task, but far from an easy one. Samuel went on to be a strong prophet. It all began with this story, this evening, this one (of four!) summons and response: "I am listening."

This response shapes the whole of this book because it is where all faithful action should begin.

Before we can take even a single step toward where God intends for us to go, before we can place the first piece of an immense puzzle, a blueprint for the kingdom of God, we must listen. As simple as that may sound, we can often struggle as much as Samuel did. Samuel, who was alone in a huge empty tent in the middle of the night, didn't do a great job of recognizing the voice of the Lord. He easily explained it away, thinking that it must have been Eli. We have many distractions and competing voices that make it hard to even single out the voice of God in our midst.

In the cacophony of distractions, the lone voice of God is easily ignored or dismissed. But God is stubborn. God wants to be heard. God calls us by name and points to us, wanting our attention from the annual budget meetings, the annual reports due, and the conference statistical analysis that was due yesterday. Beyond the veil of getting the kids to school or mowing the lawn, God is speaking. Clearing it all away is the first great hurdle toward discerning where God is calling.

But God calls you by name, and you are left to respond.

I am listening.
In the chaos of everyday life, with the dishes to be done and the dry cleaning to be picked up;
In the excitement of friendships blossoming and consuming our time and focus;
In the weight of hard decisions, loss, or illness;
In the anxiety of declining church numbers and denominational turmoil;
In the fear of letting down the church, your family, God;
I am listening.

This is where God's calling becomes direction. God goes from calling your name to giving you purpose. In Thomas Nelson's biblical interpretation The Voice, God's response to Samuel's "I'm listening," is written as, "Pay Attention! I am about to do something so amazing in Israel . . . " (1 Samuel 3:11, The Voice).

God called, Samuel prepared himself to listen, and then God did something amazing. This is both the nature of God and the nature of calling. We are invited to take part in the amazing, the awe-inspiring, the miraculous. The Bible tells story after story of ordinary people parting seas, slaying giants, and walking on water because God called them and they listened.

"Peter, get out of the boat!"
"Noah, build a boat!"
"Zacchaeus, come down!"
"Saul, get up and go!"
"Dorcas, wake up!"
"Lazarus, come out!"

If we can recognize the call and still ourselves long enough to listen, amazing things will happen. Once we hear that call and listen, we begin the work of discernment and can begin to understand where God is actually calling us to be a part of the miraculous.

Discerning

Discernment is a loaded word in the church. We throw it around in a number of contexts. Sometimes, we are talking about how we interpret God's responses to our prayers. Oftentimes, we use it when we discuss our calls into ministry or important decisions we are making in our lives or churches. It may be what we call the search for purpose when something profound happens in our lives, when circumstances require us to shift in some way. More than once I've heard the word used to gently shrug off an unwelcome idea instead of saying no.

"That's an interesting suggestion. Let's spend some time discerning if God is calling us to that particular opportunity," said every pastor.

Even in that particularly roundabout context, we get glimpses of what this word means to us in our modern world. Discernment is a specialized process in which we seek out God's plan, whether it is specifically in our lives, in the tough decisions our congregations may face, or in planning new ministries. As Christians, we should consider the big idea that God has in store for us, our ministries, our individual churches, and the global church. We should be open to that invitation for all of us to play our part in the amazing things God is doing in our midst already.

In the Wisconsin Conference of The United Methodist Church, there's a "Discernment Retreat" built into the clergy candidacy process in which we spend time reflecting on things like our faith stories, the ministries we are a part of, and why we think we are called to ministry. We start with the story of when God called us by name and we were still enough to listen to what God had to say for us. Then, we spend days learning about what the process is to become United Methodist clergy, what aspects of faith leadership do and do not require us to be clergy, and some general nuts-and-bolts discussion about our own futures leading in the church. It represents both parts of good discernment: identifying the call from God and examining and preparing for that call. You may be called to be a pastor. You may be called to be a plumber. In either case, there is a process in which we must understand the depth of that call so we can understand what God is looking for us to do.

Theologian Frederick Buechner defines vocation as the place where "your deep gladness and the world's deep hunger meet."[1] Many of us came to understand this as a foundational concept for our own call to ministry. We have a deep passion for God and ministry. The world needs people to help lead the church. Our calling is what leads us into the world as leaders, and we very likely spent time discerning that call. In many cases, we spent a long time ignoring and actively avoiding that call until finally it became necessary to sit and talk with God about it. This context of discernment, call, and purpose is likely familiar to you, and I would be willing to bet you have even read this Buechner quote along the way. What we might have overlooked is how we can use this same understanding of call and purpose for something even greater than our personal vocation. Or, equally likely, we as individual churches have become so focused on weathering institutional turmoil, recalling the past glory days, or just keeping our doors open that we've become oblivious to the calls to our church.

Your church has a deep gladness, a specific set of skills or resources that collide with the deep hunger within your community. Just like your own vocation and call, your church or ministry has a vocation and a call too. Your community has a deep need that God is already working to fill, and your ministry is called to help through its unique deep gladness. We usually have a limited organizational understanding of this through our mission and vision, as expressed by multi-paragraph statements that you compose, collect, post on your website, and promptly forget. In the best of cases, we recognize that there are very real

1. Frederick Buechner, *Wishful Thinking: A Seeker's ABC* (HarperSanFrancisco, 1993), 119.

and vital focuses on our church's purpose and future that we call mission and vision. Your church likely asked the questions at one point to discern what the church is meant to be within your local context:

What is it that this congregation meant to do?
Why this church, this community, this opportunity?
How might we do what we believe God calls us to do?

Eugene H. Peterson, in his *The Pastor: A Memoir,* said, "The vocation of pastor(s) has been replaced by the strategies of religious entrepreneurs with business plans." This displacement has affected the church's ability to divine its own vocation, distracted by formulating business plans, mission statements, and focus boards. We borrow the terms and practices from the business world to structure our organizations and often let that lead us into a secular mind-set instead of asking the simple questions of God.

Who? What? Where? How? We should be asking God these broad questions in each corner of ministry within our churches, and the Why should be apparent through it all—to build the kingdom of God. This is discernment within a church. If discernment is the faithful listening to how God answers these questions, then calling is the answer. When your congregation understands its call through discernment, your church can go forward, tackling the deep hungers within your community in a way that only your ministry can.

We are called, just like Samuel.

Called by name with a call just for you.

This is the space where a new faith expression is being planted by God.

The ground is fertile, and the need is profound.

As Samuel grew up, the Lord helped him and made everything Samuel said come true. From the town of Dan in the north to the town of Beersheba in the south, everyone in the country knew that Samuel was truly the Lord's prophet.

—1 Samuel 3:19-20 CEB

Chapter 3

Door and Radio

Open Doors

Institutional discernment—our church's understanding of God's call—is often misunderstood. We tend to view it as a binary, cause-and-effect, almost transactional process. It's crucial to step back and analyze our own assumptions and ideas about how discernment works.

I'm not particularly knowledgeable about finance, so when I have a question about my retirement investments, I call my accountant. I usually receive a specific answer, just what I am looking for. I have sometimes mistakenly assumed institutional discernment works the same way. I might approach God with a direct question like, "How can I get more young families into our congregation?" Then, faithfully listen for God to give me a clear and specific answer. Truthfully, in my earlier years, I held somewhat fantastical ideas about what this would look like: clouds parting, a booming baritone voice explaining how we should restructure Sunday school. Or a slam-dunk marketing technique to engage unchurched millennial parents. A dove descends with a list of social media posts that will inspire parents to suddenly attend our worship service, and the sun pauses in the sky to create time for the new families to worship, have coffee and muffins, and still make it to the traveling soccer game on time.

So far, that has not once been my experience with discernment.

Another example of my mistaken ideas about discernment: Sometimes I have asked for words that will inspire the congregation to increase their giving. I have prayed, "Lord, give me the phrases I need to move people into great generosity and budgets fulfilled!" Then I wait patiently in front of my laptop, ready to capture the bolt of inspiration. It would be so much easier if there were an app in which I could query God for specific answers to all my specific questions! But again, that is not how it works. God isn't a research tool, and when I fall into this pattern of thinking, I misunderstand discernment.

Maybe you, too, are prone to this misunderstanding, treating the discernment process like an on/off switch. But instead of asking a specific question and seeking a specific answer, we need to *ask God what God has in mind for us.* Think of discernment less like flipping a switch, more like opening a door.

The open door is a common metaphor for opportunity. An open door is uncontrolled. Anything could wander in or be let out. As my dad loudly warned throughout my childhood, we could let out all the heat. A door can be an exit, an entrance, a welcome, or an escape. This is how discernment actually works. We open our doors (and our minds, hearts) and ask what possibilities exist, what God has in mind for us. Instead of, "How do I attract young families?" we might ask, "Where are you calling our church to meet new people?" Instead of, "How do I get people to

16

give more money?" we might ask, "How can we use the resources God has provided to change our corner of the world?"

When we open doors, anything can and will happen. God will waltz in and out, inviting us to do the same. But to be truly open in our discernment we must lay aside our expected responses. Our approach should be more like asking for advice than seeking specific answers. This is crucial: We must step back, recognize our preconceived ideas about what is possible and what God has in mind for us. We must in genuine humility acknowledge that we often have little idea what God is doing in our midst. Think back over your life and ministry, and you'll likely remember many times when only in retrospect you were able to understand what God was up to and how God was at work around you. When we approach discernment for our churches from our deeply entrenched assumptions, with preconceived ideas about what will happen, we ask questions that are limited by design, aimed to evoke the responses we expect. When we do this, only listening for answers to our narrow questions, we are pulling the doors nearly shut, limiting our own capacity for open conversation with God, stifling the process of discernment.

Narrow, direct questions come from a specific place and lead to another specific place. They presuppose a destination. But the broadness of an open-door invitation can lead your church to anywhere God might be working. Many times, this is how miracles work in the Bible. God provides what is needed in a way that is beyond the understanding of the people present. God works through talking donkeys, never-ending flour jars, and healing handkerchiefs (Numbers 22:28; 1 Kings 17:16; Acts 19:12).

In their journey through the desert, the Israelites experienced many hardships, few as scary as the plague of venomous snakes.

Many Israelites were bitten and died, and the people came to Moses asking for him to pray for deliverance. "Pray that God takes away the snakes," they told Moses, and Moses did. In response, God instructed Moses to make a bronze snake on a pole that would heal all those bitten. God's solution was not specifically what Moses was asking, and if he had simply prayed, "God, lose the snakes. Please and thank you," then went on his merry way, nothing would have happened. Snakes would have flourished, many more Israelites would have been bitten and died, and it's possible that Moses would have begun to doubt the power of God. That doubt could have easily derailed the entire Israelite nation on their journey to the promised land, who were barely hanging on by a thread already. It's even possible the snakes would have finished off the lot of them and the trajectory of God's chosen people would have been tragically altered. Luckily, even when Moses asked for something specific on behalf of the people, he had learned enough about how God works to listen through an open door and hear the call to another solution. This is what good, open-door discernment looks like.

The process of this open-door discernment also protects us from self-oriented motives. If we are asking for a specific answer, we can approach God with our own desires, fears, and sins manifesting through our questions. If we are simply opening the door to God to speak, we aren't asking questions like, "How can I become one of those big-time pastors in the mega-churches?" Our fears of inadequacy, financial shortfalls, plummeting attendance, or job security are not where we begin in fruitful discernment or calls. Nor are the selfish desires of large crowds, fame, or power. When we begin with a self-oriented question, that question has motives. It seeks an answer that serves us. It is asking God to interact in our world in the way we desire. Even if our motives are selfless, they are still our motives, not God's. Questions can be limited, selfish, destructive, and counter-missional. Open doors are just open doors. There's nothing selfish, fearful, proud, egotistical, or manipulative about listening. When we ask God to direct us to where God wants us, our church, and our community, we open ourselves to a righteous invitation to satisfy God's desire instead of our own.

As you go through this process, it will be important to be wide open. The broader you can open up your perception to you and your institution's call, the more likely you will hear it. No one expects a talking donkey, but at least once God used one to bring God's message to people. So, before you even begin the process, open yourself up to all possibilities, and continually check yourself, drawing yourself back to this state of openness. Trust that God's advice is better than any specific answer you might be searching for.

Tuning In

God's call is also often like a radio. How many times have you turned on your radio exactly at the beginning of the song you want to hear? More often you turn it on to hear a song already playing. When we open the door to hear what God is calling us to be a part of, oftentimes we discover God is already in the middle of something miraculous that we are invited to be a part of. As churches shrink or close, the focus shifts to maintaining the institution. Churches can find themselves solely addressing the budgetary crises or the decline in attendance and giving. We can get so wrapped up in maintaining the structure and organization of the local church that we have little time to BE the church in our local community! Lucky for the community, God isn't dependent upon the church to change the world. God will go ahead and begin working on people's hearts well before the church is ready to help. So, when we finally are ready to discern where God is calling us to be, through our open-door prayers, we will very likely find the song has already begun.

I bring this up because when we are late to the party, there is a natural tension. It can be easy to dismiss the call because why would our call start without us? It is equally easy to want to step in and demand control, even though we are outsiders just beginning to experience what God is doing.

When I was in high school, my church was without any real ministry for high school students. There were many opportunities to connect with the church as a child, but when it came to post-confirmation engagement, the pickings were slim. A few key leaders underwent a process to discern God's call to discipleship and discovered that many teenagers from the church were already meeting on their own at a local coffee shop after hours, singing praise songs and talking about the Bible. Through the faithful discernment of God's call to ministry, they decided that this was something God wanted the church to help with. In this revelation, my home church didn't ignore this call because it was already happening elsewhere, assuming that it couldn't be for them. They didn't barrel into the space, trying to take over and scattering the participants in the process. Instead, they engaged the teens present and the few adults who were laterally connected and learned what God was doing there. In those conversations and the work done over the next year, a ministry emerged that led hundreds of teens to a deep faith in God. Several of my clergy friends and

I began exploring our own calls to ministry in that space. The church faithfully followed a call into a space outside their walls that ultimately built a small corner of the kingdom of God in a new and exciting way.

As you begin this process of understanding discernment and the execution of God's call, consider doors and radios. The openness with which we approach the process will define how successful we are at hearing what God is saying. The willingness and patience to explore calls that engage us with God's work already happening will lead us to new corners of the community. As difficult as it may be to approach God broadly and patiently when we feel all the pressures associated with local church leadership, if we only listen narrowly or hurriedly, we will miss the message. Discernment is hearing, examining, and wrestling with God's call. It's following where God is leading you and your church. It takes patience and wisdom, not haste. The word *discernment* comes from the Greek word *anakrino*, which means to examine or distinguish, and neither of those things is done quickly or without thought. Discernment is done properly when it is thorough. It is faithful when it is done patiently.

Open-door discernment and radio calls take a level of trust. They require that we be willing to acknowledge that God knows what's best for us, our church, the community, and the kingdom.

If any of you lacks wisdom, you should ask God, who gives generously to
all without finding fault, and it will be given to you.
But when you ask, you must believe and not doubt,
because the one who doubts is like a wave of the sea,
blown and tossed by the wind.

—James 1:5-6 NIV

Chapter 4

Beginning

In the spring of 2006, as I began my very first youth group meeting in my very first church ministry position, I discovered several things very quickly. I had spent many hours over the previous days preparing for that first meeting, planning what I thought was a solid first meeting with the students. I had mapped out down to the minute how we would move through the meeting, starting with five minutes for an ice breaker, then an activity that would involve movement because of an article I had read on the importance of physical movement in learning. I researched games for those with limited mobility and activities that would be better for unathletic teens. I researched articles about gross motor skills and fine motor skills, and ways that games can create strong neuropathways in developing minds. I read about improv games that help develop strong listening and communication skills. Then, after I was satisfied I had the best game planned out, I wrote a lesson that would take thirty minutes with discussion to round out the evening. I had spent several hours researching a Bible passage I believed to be relevant to teenage life, exhaustively pouring over Bible commentaries and reading devotionals written by my favorite Christian authors. I came up with fun, relatable illustrations to keep the interest of the teenagers as well as connect the lesson to their everyday lives. And, after it all, I had planned to close in a prayer that I had practiced and clocked in at three minutes, leaving another three minutes to clean up, finishing exactly on time. I had planned it, practiced it, and was ready to execute it with the precision of a Swiss watchmaker.

We blew through all of it in about twenty-two minutes.

In the midst of this catastrophic failure, I began to throw anything I could think of at the wall to see what would stick. It was a flurry of panic! I was trying games I had read about in my research or that I had played a decade before when I was in youth group. I expanded the lesson on the fly to include additional discussion points and got us pretty far in the weeds. I ended up with a fairly scattered, chaotic, and underdeveloped meeting. By the end, I was hoping and praying the youth would come back the next week and give me a second chance. It was not my proudest ministry moment and, as I mentioned, this episode taught me a few very important things.

First, I was terrible at guessing how long something would take. Really, really bad.

Second, during the event is exactly the wrong time to figure out what I should be doing. I needed to find a better way to figure out what this ministry was going to look like before I was already leading it.

Third, it wasn't that my level of preparation was bad, it was just incorrectly focused. I was working to fully develop my own plan instead of God's plan for this ministry meeting. I hadn't even begun to ask God what God's plan was for the ministry itself, let alone how we might move through our meeting time toward that call. As I began working within this new ministry context, I wasn't asking the right questions about the ministry and its purpose. Instead of working through a process of discernment about what

God wanted with this ministry or what God was already doing in the lives of these teens and this church community, I began to develop my own plans as thoroughly as I could. I over-prepared in so many ways but failed to ask even a single question of discernment or call.

So where should I have begun?

Whenever we begin a process to discern God's plan or purpose, it should start with prayer. Before we begin any of the actual nuts and bolts of new ministries or expressions, before we make bold decisions in our church or community, before we start the process of reflection and evaluation needed to do this correctly, before we hype it to the church and wider community, we need to talk to God. This is how I describe prayer to my congregation each Sunday morning; we must have a conversation with God, creating space for God to speak back into our lives. We ask some stuff and then we listen. In this context, we ask God some questions and then we wait for God to speak up.

Guessing what God wants is not what discernment is, though that is exactly what happens sometimes in our ministries and churches. We decide what God wants based on dozens of arbitrary factors—what we have done in the past, what other local churches are doing, what we just read somewhere in a book or online. And sometimes we don't even think about God at all in these decisions. We decide what to do based on what we think we're good at, or on our own personal tastes and preferences, or on the new cool ministry fad. We do things because of mandates from our denomination or church organization higher-ups. But, regardless of how successful or fruitful these decisions might turn out to be, they lack the one crucial insight: nobody asked God. As my dad used to say, "Even a blind squirrel finds a nut every once in a while." Applying that pearl of wisdom, even the undiscerned ministry offering may bear fruit, bring in new people, and share the gospel once in a while. But we can do far better than blind squirrels; God is actively waiting to show us the way if only we will ask and listen.

"God, what drives our faith community?"
"God, where are people in unanswered need around us?"
"God, where are you already working in our midst? How can we be a part of it?"
"God, how can we be good stewards of our time and resources?"
"God, why me? Why now? Why here?"
"God, what are we being called to do?"

Ask God where to begin, where to go from here, where God wants you to end up; any insight that you can gather from God is more valuable than all the market research, crowdsourcing, and innovation *you* could do. Market research, crowdsourcing, and innovation are all important as we will discuss soon enough, but they should not be our starting point. On the one hand, our decision-making is often clouded by ambition, fear of failure, and the very attractive paths of least resistance. God's wisdom, on the other hand, is the voice of truth. It is our job to receive that truth and execute it faithfully.

That is the other part of prayer as part of discernment: asking God for the wisdom to learn all you can from those call questions, interpreting what you learn and designing a plan accordingly, and implementing the plan as best you and your congregation can.

Ask God for the ears to hear God's nudging in this process.

Ask God for eyes to see the Holy Spirit moving in your community.

Ask for help understanding what God might be planning with this opportunity.

Ask for God's patience when you screw it all up and need to start over.

And over, and over, and over . . .

If I had done this with my first ministry—asking for help from God to understand our collective call within our context and for the wisdom to listen and understand what God had planned—that first year of ministry would have looked very different.

We got there eventually. Enough stuck to the walls in those chaotic first meetings to ensnare the hearts of spiritually hungry teenagers. That bought me enough time to develop some stronger prayer habits and learn all about discernment. And over the next six years, we would grow into a vibrant, faith-filled set of three age-level ministries with strong focuses on spiritual development and discipleship. We saw fruit in ways that the church had never seen before, sparking teenagers and young adults to serve in the church, move on to lead in other congregations, and even go into ministry leadership themselves. And the only way we could do that was to begin by asking God's opinion before we started doing our own things.

Prayer creates a space for God to speak and guide. It is through prayer that church leaders communicate with God and take the time to pause and listen. As we should do in our own prayer life, discernment happens with plenty of space for God to speak back to us. It must be a conversation, in which both parties can come together. So, in our prayerful discernment, we as leaders must faithfully listen before we act, and it must be an ongoing process as we seek to discern God's will for the church or our ministry.

Coming to God first in prayer can only work if we are asking for the right thing. As the author of *Flood Gates*, Sue Nilson Kibbey put it at the 2018 NYAC United Methodist Laity Convocation, "Pray to God to do a new thing, not to bless the same old, same old. Don't just ask God to bless what you have planned, ask God to show us the new hopes and dreams. Let's move the church to look up and out." We must be willing to ask the tough question, *What new thing might our church be capable of?* Or, perhaps even more difficult, the question, *What thing are we doing that no longer bears fruit?* These questions are scary to ask, because if you listen, God will absolutely answer them. There is somewhere your church isn't reaching that God is calling you to reach. There very well may be something in your church that has passed its time of effectiveness and is now ready to be phased out. Prayer to God in times of discernment means asking for the tough answers and listening with open ears.

Even though I can look back at this with all the wisdom I've achieved over the decades since then, I don't want you to get the wrong idea. After almost two decades of youth ministry, pastoral and congregational ministry, event planning, worship planning, new faith expressions, and ministry consulting work, I still mess up my time budgeting. I still make those rookie mistakes like that first youth meeting. I have moments that I find myself reeling because I've run out of time and have too much material, or run out of material with plenty of time left. But, in those moments of quick, fly-by-the-seat-of-my-pants leadership, I am able to approach the situation with a better idea of what God has in mind for this opportunity because of the discernment process my leadership team and I have undertaken together. I have already asked for God's guidance and patience. I've done the leg work of meeting with God and gathering the tools around me to make better decisions that lead me toward where God intends.

Go where your best prayers take you.

—Frederick Buechner, *Telling Secrets: A Memoir*

Chapter 5

Examine Your Context

If the first step of discernment is to ask God the guiding questions in prayer, then the second step of this process is to paint yourself a detailed picture of your context so that the answers to those prayers make sense. When we reach out to God in prayer, especially prayers of discerning God's plan, we will get an answer if we listen correctly. But listening and hearing is only half the battle. We should always go into prayer with an expectation that God will be both present and participatory, while also understanding that an important part of communication is our own ability to contextualize what we are hearing. It's like that friend of yours who speaks primarily in movie and television quotes. If you haven't seen the movie, it's hard to understand what your pal is trying to say. Knowing your context intimately helps to understand your church's call more fully.

You may reside in the community where your church is located, and in this case you'll be leading the institutional discernment process with an advantage. It is easier to understand the rhythms and flow of the people who live in a community when you live there too. Living in your geographical ministry area gives you a view from street level, because you are the boots on the ground. It's easier to answer the question, *What deep need is within this community?* when you also are within the community, because you may experience the deep need firsthand. You see the breakdown in the community systems. You hear the grumblings at the grocery store. You witness the interactions of community members at their kids' school events or how they treat one another at town council meetings. You are in situations outside of your structured ministerial obligations and interactions, which lead you to new insights you can't simply glean from behind the pulpit on a Sunday morning.

If you don't live within the community you serve in your ministry, you must be even more deliberate in understanding the context, putting yourself into those unstructured situations, and observing people outside of their church personas. It takes time and consideration to execute. Eat out at local restaurants often, get your groceries in town before driving home, or join a local club or league. Create for yourself opportunities to see the community from outside your church office window.

And understand that, even if you live in the community, you are not going to be privy to every need and happening within that community. You are just one person with one point of view in a complex community system, making it nearly impossible for you to fully understand the new places God is calling you and the church. So how do you paint an accurate picture of your context? And what does that picture represent?

Both Sides of the Equation

In algebra, one of the first foundational principles taught is that there are two sides of an equation, and that there is a balance between them. Both are part of the other, but both are on opposing sides of the problem. In the same way, your context has two balanced sides—inside the church and outside the church. Inside the church is the culmination of tradition, culture, quirk, and personality, while outside the church is the local cultural structure in which the church currently exists.

In the healthiest and most fruitful of balances, the inside church culture and ethos serve and connect with the outside church community in a way that connects people with God. This is where the church's mission and vision are in line with what God is calling the church to do and be. The congregation and leadership are working to align the church structures, ministries, and events with the mission and vision, and the community is being engaged and supported faithfully. This leads to church growth, lives changed, and kingdoms built. In less fruitful times, there is an imbalance that must be corrected to make the equation work.

So, before anything can be started, stopped, modified, or augmented, you need to understand where everything is beginning. Start with your church or ministry.

Ask yourself,

What is the purpose of the organization?

What makes it special? Why does it exist?

What are its idiosyncrasies? How has it grown and been shaped into what it is now?

How does it interact with people within the organization? People outside the organization?

Why do people join? Why do people leave?

What resources does this organization have at its disposal? A building? Green space? Staff? Existing missions and outreaches?

What is the reputation of this organization within the wider community? Is it accurate? Why is it portrayed this way?

There are dozens of questions to answer and facets to define, so spend the time to look at it from as many angles as possible so that you can begin to understand the identity of the church as it relates to itself, to the community, to its members, and to God.

Then begin to approach the community in the same way. Begin asking yourself questions that lead to an understanding of the unique identity of the community.

What does the community look like ethnically? Religiously? Economically?

Where do people shop? Eat? Live?

Where do people work? What is the employment rate in town?

What are people worried about within the community? Excited about? Passionate about?

Where are current churches and ministries connecting with people? Where are they missing?

In seminary, I worked under Dr. Chris James, author of *Church Planting in Post-Christian Soil*. In his Gospel in Context classes, we worked to exegete a neighborhood to try to understand where the gospel existed within that context already. Part of the work was to ask these questions over and over, to people who lived and worked in the community and to other community leaders, and to try to experience the findings through our own eyes. We also compiled demographic data and economic surveys and tracked growth sectors over the previous decades. But the exegetical work was incomplete. We also physically walked through the community, observing and digesting what we could see, hear, and feel. The culture and context are the adjectives of the community, describing what it is and transforming your understanding of your community from flat into three dimensions.

At my current church, this understanding of the community led to one of the best marketing and outreach opportunities we've had in the church's history. A local event at a bowling alley was cancelled due to possible community backlash. After talking to the bowling alley management, we learned that much of the pressure was coming from individuals from outside our geographic location, and the possible backlash were specific to that venue. We deemed that the event aligned with our own mission and vision, and we weighed the consequences of hosting the event differently. After some discernment and prayer, we decided to host the event ourselves at our location. It was a last-minute scenario, so the event was small and simple, only doing what we believed we could do well. It was the talk of the town. Local businesses and pillars of the community had been very vocal in their disappointment in the event being cancelled originally, and so they were in turn very vocal in support of the church hosting. It led to dozens of business partnerships and connections, large-scale organic publicity within the community, and touch points with dozens of new families, a target growth demographic for our congregation.

It was the avenue in which many seeds were planted within our wider community in ways we are still just beginning to realize. Had we not been in touch with the local context and what was happening around us, this opportunity would have likely passed us by.

Two things to note about this example:

First, as previously mentioned, your view shouldn't be the only view of the community because it is too narrow to get a fair and robust profile of the broader culture. This event's discernment did not happen in a vacuum; the leadership board, a group of staff members, and a dedicated group of laity were all involved in the discernment and execution of this event, each playing a pivotal role in how we planned the event itself so that it connected with all the people it was meant to connect with. People from within the church should be helping you develop this understanding of context. Bring others into this evaluative effort so that you don't miss opportunities or botch an amazing opportunity.

Second, your church and your community are both living, changing systems. and your contextual awareness of their identities will have to be ongoing. Like a well-balanced ecosystem, new additions to the congregation will have an effect on the culture. The event we undertook in this instance had a very specific context with the cancellation of a similar event making news in the wider community. If we hadn't had that setup, the event wouldn't have had the traction or reaction within the community it had. We couldn't do this event a year later with the same impact. Contexts and situations change. World events will trickle down into your local community. Even when you have that perfect inside/outside church balance, it is not static. You have to shift, grow, and change as fluidly as the rest of the world does to maintain that balance. You must have your fingers on the collective pulse of the church and your ear to the ground to know what is new in your community surroundings. These changes are crucial to know when a ministry needs to shift or to end gracefully, and can often illuminate the newest opportunities for your church to partner with God in what God is doing in your midst.

The church of tomorrow will be much more engaged in addressing the needs of the community. This church will be known more for its members' relational acts of compassion outside of the church walls—taking ministry out, rather than waiting for outsiders to come in and sit.

—Linda Ranson Jacobs,
*Attract Families to Your Church
and Keep Them Coming Back*

Chapter 6

Gather and Trust

Discernment is a unique experience. There are many ways that God speaks into our lives, and there are many ways that God may present or verify a call into your or your church's life. For Rev. Ben Johnston-Krase, it was a dream. One night, while serving as the pastor of First Presbyterian Church in Racine, Wisconsin, Ben had a dream where he was the pastor of a new church, but there was no church building—only a farm. The dream had him waking up excited, which led him downstairs to his computer where he googled "Farm Church." He was excited to read about who was out there doing this cool thing and wanting to learn more, only to find zero results. No one was doing anything that resembled this Farm Church dream that had woken him up and quickened his pulse. Chasing that feeling and impulse, in the middle of the night, alone at his computer, he went to GoDaddy and purchased the domain name FarmChurch.org.

In the morning, Ben told his wife about the dream and the beginning stages of his discernment around it: the shadow of a mission and vision to worship and grow food to share it with the community. She heard his words and shared his vision, and the journey began. The discernment process for this new faith expression started in the kitchen, with Ben and his wife fleshing out the groundwork.

Discernment is as unique as the people and communities that undergo the discernment. Sometimes God shouts at you from parted clouds. Sometimes God gives you a dream to nudge you into the right space. Many times, God pokes you right in the back of your brain when an opportunity presents itself. In all these cases, there is a procedure in which you can take the beginning of the process—pronouncement from heaven, disrupting dream, not-so-subtle nudge in your brain—and carry it into faithful execution. These steps help to organize the process of taking an idea and developing it into something meaningful and to give it the organizational support to thrive.

Gather a Team

Pastor Ben Johnston-Krase began the very first step that first morning when he cast the (incomplete) vision to his wife and brought her into the discernment; he began gathering a team. He then reached out to seminary friends and colleagues Allen Brimer and Brandon Wert and shared the vision with them. They immediately felt Ben's passion and call from God and replied, "We're in!" The team was set, Ben the vision caster, Allen Brimer the person with the farming experience, and Brandon Wert the person with community-organizing passion and experience. They identified the corners of this idea, defined the basic structure and needs of this idea, and gathered people to begin the discernment and planning.

When you begin to have a vision, a thought, or an idea, gather those who will be part of this expression to begin developing it. Too many expressions fully ordained by God die because of poor planning or being launched half-baked. A team of people who are also called to be involved with this discerned idea, working together to develop this idea into a well-executed expression, are invaluable. It is often what takes a calling into something more, something profound, because the calling isn't enough. The calling is where we are invited to be a partner in the process, and if you've ever worked in school in a group project, you know how crucial it is that everyone does their part. Gather a team and develop every piece of your new idea so that you can have the best chance for success. Reflect during the planning, executing, and refining stages of the expression with the team. Take the time to do it right, and do it together.

Trust the Vision

Ben took a sabbatical in 2014 without a home for this visionary expression. He dove into the development of Farm Church and began a nation-wide search for the right community and context for this idea. From California to New York, the team considered characteristics and locations, seeking God's guidance throughout the process. The team felt God drawing them toward Durham, North Carolina. It was a good space for the new expression, with its extreme need for food security and vast food deserts. In August 2015, the team moved their families across the country to Durham, without complete funding or a congregation. In 2023, Farm Church was established in the Durham community, battling food insecurity, worshipping, and building the kingdom of God faithfully. It all happened because this team of faithful leaders trusted God in their discernment and followed where the vision led.

This is possibly the scariest part of the process. God calls people into unlikely, unfamiliar, sometimes unimaginable spaces. Discerning those calls is difficult enough, but then we must follow with a heart that trusts that God is calling us to the place we will best serve the kingdom of God.

Leaving behind convention is hard.

Leaving behind tradition is harder.

Convincing others to follow and trust might be the hardest of all.

Part of acknowledging God's call in your life is trusting that God got it right.

As iron sharpens iron, so one person sharpens another.

—Proverbs 17:27

Chapter 7

Let the Laity Loose

In 2011, I became the solo pastor of a smaller rural Methodist church in a wider community that had collectively forgotten that there was a Methodist church in town. In the decades previous, as I was often reminded by the most senior generation in the congregation, the church had birthed a ministry called "Ready Kids for School" in which the community came together to provide supplies for local underprivileged students that had since grown to give out clothing and supplies to hundreds. The ministry outgrew what the church could handle running and struck out on its own. My smaller rural church struggled to remain a relevant part of the ministry. In an effort to do so, I called the director and asked what specific gaps in donations they had, so we could rally our limited resources and fill one of those gaps. Without hesitation she said, "Underwear." People often remembered to donate pencils, notebooks, folders, and crayons, but at the end of the event, the biggest need left unfulfilled was clean, new underwear. So, our small congregation had an "Undie Sunday" in which we collected over one thousand pairs of brand-new underwear for children, connecting us as an important part of this powerful mission.

The following Sunday I shared how many pairs we were able to collect and invited the congregation to imagine the students who would now be able to approach their first day of school with a complete set of new clothes, knowing how uncomfortable and self-conscious one can be in worn-out clothes. I mentioned how confident I imagined the children could feel in the clothes they would be wearing, giving them a boost for their new school year. After service, one of the congregants came up to me and said the last line really got her thinking. As a stylist, she was inspired to think about haircuts and how a good haircut can make all the difference on a high-stress day like the first day of school. She spent the rest of the service thinking about it and discerning God's call to this specific need in the community and finally brought it to me as a possible mission idea. There were several other stylists within the congregation who were willing to donate their time as well as a salon owner who graciously donated four salon chairs and goodie bags of hair care products. That first year, this event served over twenty-five families with almost forty appointments, giving students a fresh haircut for their first day of school. To this day, this mission event was one of the most interesting, well-executed events I have been a part of, and it wasn't my idea at all. Glenda Sue, a layperson, was the mastermind and point person in the discernment process.

This has actually been true for many of my favorite events, missions, and outreaches over the years. As clever, smart, innovative, or lucky as I think I am, or as in touch as I think my discernment efforts have been as a pastor, some of the most fruitful endeavors I have been a part of have come from laypeople who were listening to where God is calling their church. It would be easy to make the mistake of assuming discernment is best left to the professionals, or that leadership holds the only connection point with God's vision for the church. The institution the wider church has become is often structured and built from the top down, so it would be easy to make that same mistake and think that somehow the denomination or the pastor or the church elders have the direct pipeline to God's call for the local church. That would be easy to think but is absurd. Laity are in the community in a different way than local clergy. They live the context differently and see God moving in their midst differently.

The members of your ministry have eyes, ears, and hearts for all different corners of your community and will have a richer understanding of the deep needs within that community. And just like the leadership, there is a divine connection between the individual and the Creator in which laypeople can discern calls upon their lives and their church. To think that we have the monopoly on ideas and calls from God is to undervalue our greatest resource as a worshipping community—our people. God created a diverse, nuanced, and complicated body, and we all have a part to play in this church and kingdom. God is actively calling the laity into new, exciting spaces for Jesus. In fact, God is probably calling the laity into specific new spaces that only those laity can occupy well. God may be calling the laity to lead their church into spaces that the clergy feels ill-equipped, undereducated, or downright awkward about going. Clergy must relinquish control and empower others through this process.

Finding the Sweet Spot

Sometimes, we do a good job of releasing laypeople but bumble the opportunities in other ways. We as leaders should work alongside laity as facilitators of the discernment process and implementation. There is a sweet spot between gatekeeping the divine inspiration of discernment and releasing all involvement to the laypeople. Somewhere between thinking we alone are the origin of all things visionary or discernable within our church and the antithetical throwing up of our hands and shouting, "I wash my hands of this," we find space to serve as nurturer and facilitator of the calls for the congregation. When people like Glenda Sue come to us with something that they believe is God-inspired, we should meet it first with the expectation that it holds true to our church's mission and vision, and then we should ask, "How can the church help you lead this? How can I help you follow this call?"

All endeavors through your organization should hold up to that scrutiny—that there is an easily articulatable connection with the mission and vision of your organization. Once that is verified, you become the chief facilitator, empowering the laity to lead, cast vision, and exercise passion, all within an organizational structure. You help facilitate the planning, preparation, organization, and execution of the event. This is what it looks like to let your laity loose, empowered to do what they are called to do through the church, but focused enough to do it well.

It's not micro-management of the laity or the Holy Spirit.

It's also not letting chaos reign.

It's trusting that God has a vision too big for just you to carry and faithfully embracing the diversity of creation in your local context.

What It All Looks Like

In the midst of the COVID-19 shutdown, when the church wasn't meeting in-person and most of our ministries were on hold, I got a call from a peripheral church member who had in the past several years been attending another church. She asked me, "Have you ever heard of Ruby's Pantry?" I had not, and she went on to rapidly and enthusiastically explain that Ruby's Pantry is a food-share program designed to combat food insecurity in the Midwest. She went on to say that the program would be perfect for our region, a community that was struggling through the pandemic, and that this would be a perfect opportunity for our church to execute its mission and vision. When she finally paused to take a breath, it was evident that she was deep in the process of discernment. Her own deep gladness had aligned with our church's deep gladness and intersected with the deep needs related to food insecurity in our community. She had done the foot work and asked the "Why now, why us, why here?" questions and was ready to collaborate in the discernment. She invited me to ask those questions too. After my own discernment and reflection, I asked, "How can the church help you lead this?" We were able to recruit a team of volunteers to facilitate the new missional expression, partner with the community and local resources, visit other Ruby's Pantry sites to learn from their experiences, adapt to our context and skills, and ultimately build what we believed God had called us to build.

This Ruby's Pantry site started with 350 shares that first month, able to accommodate a maximum of 350 households. We learned from some system failings and details we had overlooked at that first event, and the next month we served more shares in less time. Each time we met as a board, we spent time reflecting on what we believed God wanted us to accomplish and how we could do that better, faster, or bigger next time. Within three months, we had become the largest Ruby's site in Wisconsin, serving over 600 shares through a small army of volunteers from the church and wider community. Within another two months, we had become the largest Ruby's site in existence at the time, with 750 shares. That means that 750 food-insecure households from all around Southern Wisconsin had a pantry full of food because of the diligent work of a few laypeople following God's call. We worked hard to execute each month better than the previous, keeping wait times as low as possible, moving cars as efficiently as possible, and always approaching debriefing meetings with an attitude of openness to what God might be inspiring us to do differently.

My job as the pastor throughout was to speak on behalf of the church's mission and vision and to continually ask the question, "How can the church help you lead this?" I didn't take over or lead the team. I didn't muscle in and force my own ideas on the group. Most months, my only job was to show up on the day and run one of multiple groups of volunteers, and that was less because I am the pastor and more because of my previous experience running volunteers at these types of events. I partnered with laity to discern a call to the ministry of Ruby's Pantry in our local community and stayed true to that partnership as it thrived.

When this is all done well, new expressions can do so much more. When we unleash the laity with full support and trust of the faith community to follow where God leads, the results are nothing short of miraculous. That first full year with Ruby's, our church's statistical report showed a larger missional impact from our single congregation through this single outreach effort than the entire Annual Conference of Wisconsin the previous year— more than four hundred Methodist churches across the state. This was so remarkable, I called the statistician to verify I hadn't made a mistake on the reporting form! During a global pandemic, this site processed over half a million dollars of food, distributed to hundreds of households, connected with over a hundred volunteers from every corner of the community, and partnered with a half-dozen other food pantries and government programs on a monthly basis, all beginning with a layperson who felt the call from God to connect her great gladness with the church to the deep need within the community.

God took hold of this new missional expression and multiplied it over and over, leading to new relationships with nonprofits and pantries to create an even wider net of support for the community's hunger needs. God called, God nurtured, and God multiplied. The laity brought the church along for the ride, and the world was changed. A little corner of the kingdom of God was built.

When it works, it really works.

So Christ himself gave the apostles, the prophets, the evangelists, the pastors and teachers, to equip his people for works of service, so that the body of Christ may be built up until we all reach unity in the faith and in the knowledge of the Son of God and become mature, attaining to the whole measure of the fullness of Christ.

—Ephesians 4:11-13

Chapter 8

Not All Roads Lead to Rome

As you might have gathered, I love telling stories. I tell stories to answer questions; I tell stories to recap my day; sometimes I even tell stories to introduce the background of the stories I actually want to tell, and then I tell those stories. I feel like I am always telling stories! This is both a great tool in my preaching and one of the bigger complications in writing a book of this nature. Stories of very specific faith expressions, like the one about Ruby's Pantry, are helpful and instructive, sometimes even inspiring. When you read or hear such stories, you must also consider the process of discernment that came before and the context of that particular place in its people.

Otherwise, you might forget an important point: not every expression of faithful ministry—even remarkably successful ones being done in your community—is right for your church. You have a unique set of skills as a community, resources at your disposal, and a particular call, mission, vision, and motivation. Without understanding the WHY an expression is being done, the WHERE it is being done, and the HOW it is connecting to the particular context, it's simply a story. And, without explicitly naming those components, it is possible that readers can be misled into believing that the stories are a prescription for a successful new faith expression. Stories can only be as helpful as the reason they're told.

That being said, let me tell you another story!

Go to the Bar

When Pastor Trevor Vaughn started seminary, he was working as a construction worker, much to the confusion and amusement of his coworkers. They would take opportunities on the job site to ask him questions in a familiar and informal setting about faith, God, and the church, by sharing stories. Some stories were filled with joy, but many more were filled with pain around organized religion. Trevor would invite them to his church again and again, with the consistent response, "F*** no."

This is the context that Trevor began to discern a call to connect with these construction workers. How could he be in faithful relationship with these workers who were so colorfully articulate about never darkening the doorstep of a church again? The thirst was there; these men were constantly asking Trevor faith questions, curious to explore the divine as it intersected their world and their lives. The deep desire was there with Trevor, a seminary student who had already acknowledged and begun to develop his pastoral call. The pieces were all present, and it was just a matter of discerning what God had in mind.

Trevor asked his coworkers to connect with him to chat further after work, outside of the church. "Let's go to the bar," one construction worker offered. Trevor, a well-practiced beer drinker, gladly accepted, and that is where it all began. Eventually they began to structure the casual hangouts, calling it "Bibles and Brews," and a few construction folk began to come out. Trevor had to follow where the Spirit was leading, because this was a group of people intently avoiding organized religion. After a few gatherings of the Bibles and Brews crew, they were connected with the bar regulars as well. People overheard some of the conversation, saw the comradery, and began to be drawn to what was happening there. Not long after, Trevor jumped on an advertised community request from a local nonprofit working with housing insecurity called HEAL House for delivering sandwiches to thirty homeless people. He offered out on social media free beer from a pastor if people would come and make a peanut butter and jelly sandwich at Zoo Bar in Indianola, Iowa. He strategically planned it for the next Bibles and Brews meeting and the response was overwhelming. Over forty people showed up, about seven hundred sandwiches were made, and well over forty beers were drunk.

The opportunity grew to over one hundred sandwiches weekly, and meeting this missional opportunity was the catalyst to expand the original Bible and Brews into a new faith expression called Bar+Church. This faith expression met in local bars and met people who were not comfortable in a formal religious facility. Bar+Church gave these people space to grow in faith and to begin to heal through their religious trauma, all while providing fellowship with other believers and a missional opportunity to make a real impact in their local community. It had relationship-building, healing, fellowship, mission outreach, and faith sharing, and it was growing. Through Pastor Vaughn's faithful discernment and the guidance of the Holy Spirit, this expression took off and began living into the kingdom of God in a new way, all by going to the bar.

One of the most powerful parts of this story about Bar+Church is hearing Pastor Trevor Vaughn talk about the connection, hurt, and healing he can be a part of. He says, "You have to be good at apologizing for things you didn't do wrong, because you represent the church that has done great harm." He goes on to say that you also get really good at giving hugs. This ministry has borne fruit, worked to heal broken people, built the kingdom of God, and also has not led to any local church growth. Pastor Trevor is not working to funnel participants to his church's Sunday services or other ministries. That is not what Bar+Church is all about, and that works for this specific context and this specific expression. There's no bait and switch; it is what it is and presents itself to be.

Don't Go to the Bar

Bar+Church has caught on and spread to a few different locations under different leaders who feel called to be in this space of mission, outreach, fellowship, and healing. In each case, it begins with discernment and relationships with the people within the community. And, in each of these cases, they were born out of an existing relationship with a clergy person at a Methodist church. What this means is that at some point, the clergy person leading these new expressions is reappointed to a new location and new context, and the expression is left to continue on itself. In one such case, this meant a church member stepped in and ran their local version of Bar+Church. Her transition into the local church was smooth. She was a talented leader and charismatic speaker but was not particularly called to be leader of Bar+Church, which was her responsibility now that the founding pastor had been reappointed. In this transition, the ministry went from being an organic, inspired expression of a called leader and community to a structured, inauthentic execution by a well-meaning leader. The moment had passed, and the expression began to wilt.

The Bar+Church story highlights faithful discernment and also illustrates that not every context is ready to go to the bar. Not every expression works in every context. Though this particular faith expression might sound like a fun way to meet new people, God might not be calling you to it right now. Your church or ministry may not have a leader called into this space or who is comfortable in a bar. You may not have a community that has a bar culture that is conducive to faith expressions in its midst. You may not be in a space where your congregation is comfortable or ready to bridge to this area of the local community. And, as in the case of Bar+Church, even in a context where this specific expression may have worked at one point, it didn't always continue to work. These are all reasons not go to the bar, and that is okay. That is being faithful to your own context, church identity, and unique call as a ministry and church.

Maybe Go to the Bar

The WHY of this new faith expression originally was to create faith community with people who would otherwise not find themselves in a more formal church space. The WHERE is first at a construction site and then a bar, in a community where there was a strong bar culture and the need to reach people who were part of that bar culture, giving them a space to heal and grow as children of God. The HOW was a leader discerning the Holy Spirit's call to reach these people in a way that he was particularly and deeply connected to. The faithful replication of the expression was due to bringing in a team of people who felt similarly called and shared the practices of the original Bar+Church. It won't work just anywhere, but it also won't fail everywhere. Bar+Church now has a network of new expressions across several communities.

No story about discernment or expressions should be considered an absolute; your context has unique needs that are different from some churches and similar to others. There are both unique and similar resources available to similar organizations. There are multiple churches that have similar calls and missions within their local community while also being called into completely unique spaces too. God may very well be calling you to a similar faith expression in your context. The challenge is to faithfully discern what God is calling you to do and not be swayed by the success of other ministries or churches. Just because it works for Pastor Vaughn doesn't mean it will work for you. But maybe it will. A wave of trainings, workshops, consultations, and seminars are being put on to educate about "Fresh Expressions" in the modern church exactly like Bar+Church. But without God calling you into these specific faith expressions and the proper execution, it might be more of a drain of time, resources, and volunteers than something that brings glory to God. Not all roads lead to Rome, and not all new expressions work everywhere, so you need to be willing to take the time to map your course properly.

So, take the time to discern. Even with a compelling story or exciting idea, following the path of discernment is crucial. It's possible it would work for you, but not guaranteed. Start with your context and discernment and let an idea emerge; don't start with an idea and make it fit. Maybe go to the bar, but only if God is calling you to the bar. Discernment is the key, not an afterthought.

The church should be extra cautious about franchised formulas, since churches that are committed to bringing about change are shaped by the context in which they are birthed.

—Eddie Gibbs, *Church for Every Context: An Introduction to Theology and Practice*

Chapter 9
Size Matters

Elisha had many students at this time. Many sought being a prophet's student, and it was helpful to have a large group. Traveling was safer and the nights were definitely more lively. There was much hope with so many wishing to be trained by a faithful servant of God. But, with a group this size, sometimes lodging became an issue. Sometimes after a journey, it was nice to spread out and have your own space, which was the opposite at the school in Gilgal.

One student, emboldened by the attention of the others, called to Elisha, "Elisha! This place is getting to be too crowded! Let us go to Jordan Valley. There's space there for us to build a house for us to stay!" It was best to approach Elisha with a solution to your problem at hand.

Elisha, as stoic and impassive as ever, looked up at the boy with plain eyes. After an appraising moment, he returned his eyes to his work and simply said, "Go." The servant didn't need to be told twice. He grabbed the ax he had borrowed to collect wood and a wineskin, called to his friends who were waiting at the edge of earshot, and set off to Jordan Valley. But before the group had even left the school, the crowd stopped, one of them looking back at the prophet. The man called out, "Elisha! Please come with us!" The crowd, who had been laughing and jeering, fell silent at the invitation, all turning to see what their teacher would do. The invitation must have surprised Elisha, because his eyes turned to the students, wide and round. But the surprise only lasted a moment, and, after another appraising moment, Elisha rose and, with a nod, followed behind the eager crowd as they set out for Jordan.

When they arrived at the spot, the students began to gather wood to build the new lodge. The site was flat and good for building with a broad river a short ways off. Elisha, who had stopped walking at the edge to the clearing, stood and observed, leaning on a large branch he had found on the way. Though they had grown tired on the journey, there was a renewed energy as the students whooped and laughed, preparing the site for a new structure. There were several trees large enough to use for the building and the young man who had borrowed the ax began his solitary work, since he would not let the borrowed ax out of his sight. Cutting down trees was hard work, and the wood wasn't yielding without a fight. Soon the man was wet with sweat, swinging the ax with all his might. Suddenly the ax head flew off and fell into the rushing waters of the river. He cried out in dismay, "Oh no, Master Elisha! It was borrowed!"

The ax had been borrowed from a laborer who relied on that tool to do his work. Tools were not easy to come by, and the loss of this ax would be a devastating blow to him. It was possible it would be an end to the man's livelihood.

Elisha looked at the distressed young prophet and asked, "Where did it fall?" and the young man pointed to the spot, between two rocks in the raging waters. Without missing a beat, Elisha threw his leaning stick into the water right at that very place. The others had gathered at the shore to see, wondering what Elisha would do with the stick and impressed he could hurl it with such accuracy. Without waiting, Elisha turned and began walking back to the clearing, saying, "Go retrieve the head." Miraculously, as he said this, the ax head immediately floated to the surface and the man was able to retrieve it. The young men were amazed and relieved, witnessing this miracle of the floating ax. They were again reminded that Elisha was truly a man of God, and their faith in him deepened even more.

This miracle is one of the more unique interactions between God and humanity. When the word *miracle* is said, it conjures memories of parting the Red Sea, manna raining down from heaven, and the sun being halted in the sky. The words *acts of God* tend to bring association with the destruction of Sodom and Gomorrah or the Nile turning to blood. Grandiose events are what we remember when we think of God interacting with the world.

It's not often we reference the miracle of the floating ax in our liturgies. I would be willing to bet you've never seen it displayed in stained glass in a sanctuary.

But God made the iron ax head float in that raging river. God worked through Elisha to help the young man who borrowed the ax and the ax owner. Through this miracle, a man was spared the task of telling a friend they lost a prized possession, and that friend was spared the burden the tool loss would be. In the scope of the biblical narrative, this was not a profound miracle. To us as readers of the Bible, this hardly seems like something to use the same word as God creating a giant pillar of fire. To those two men, however, this was a huge deal.

God calls people to be a part of the miraculous, but too often we only listen for the size of miracle we think God is calling us to. It can be easy to dismiss what God could be calling your church to because you think it's too big to handle or too small to matter.

When we are asking God for something to move in our midst, when our church is struggling, we are looking for a big answer. But sometimes the answer is something small, like an ax in the stream. Other times, we may have some free time or are looking for something manageable to take into the world. In either case, we seek confirmation of a specific direction instead of listening for whatever God is planning. None of these chapters are meant to be prescriptive as to what you should or should not try. Rather, each chapter should help dissolve a filter that we employ to limit what we expect God to say. Each time we set parameters on our call, focusing only on what we think we are capable of, we risk ignoring exactly what God is calling us to do or be.

Nothing Too Small

A pastor friend recently felt a call and began to discern creating a divorce care group for his community. He has been through two divorces himself and spent much of his career counseling couples through their marriages and their divorces. It seemed like God was pointing to his unique ability to be a force of healing from empathy and experience. The church leadership had mixed feelings. The congregation had been in a spot of small growth and some leaders believed that the pastor's time was better spent on something that would bring in more people. The other leaders trusted that if God was in this call, that even though there were only one or two recently divorced people in the congregation, God would bring in droves of new people in need of support and community. In the end, they were able to come together and trust that God would provide church revival through the dozens— maybe hundreds—of people this outreach group could draw in.

The church advertised the group in the community with fliers and social media posts in neighborhood groups, announced it weeks in advance at the church, and prepared for the great multitude to arrive. And, on that Monday evening, when the doors opened, there was six people ready to join in community together around the trauma of divorce. Even after several weeks of meeting and continued promotions, the group's numbers remained small. The sanctuary was not suddenly filled with the recently divorced. This ministry impacted the lives of a total of six adults and their collective four children.

And the pastor couldn't have been happier.

God's call to create this group blossomed into a space where several families who were going through a traumatic event were able to do so together. The children became friends, able to share what they were going through with other kids who understood. The parents could vent about what was weighing on them, their fears and doubts, and in a few cases, confront the dark thoughts they were beginning to harbor. This ministry very likely saved lives. This impact, though numerically small, was life changing for the individuals who were a part of it.

God calls churches to small miracles every day, and if we're open enough to listen, plan, and execute, we, too, can experience the incredible impact a floating ax can bring.

Go Big

When I first interviewed for my youth ministry position at my second church, a youth present in the interview had noticed on my resume that I had gone to college to be a music teacher and asked me what my favorite instrument was. I had no idea that this question would become such a loaded one! I told her that though I had learned all of the traditional band and orchestra instruments, that I had taken up ukulele a few years previous and enjoyed it the most. Her immediate response was, "Cool! You should teach me!" I chuckled and redirected the conversation, making sure not to make promises before I was hired. Shortly after, the church offered me the position and I began to make arrangements to move, set up my office, and get started. That conversation about ukuleles stuck with me, and I felt called to revisit it with that student. So at my first youth group meeting after getting that position, I asked her if she really did want to learn, and if anyone else in the group wanted to learn, I'd help them get affordable ukuleles and teach a beginner's class. A few youth seemed interested, so I made up a sign-up form online and emailed it to students and their parents. This would be an easy win for me, connecting with a small group of students right off the bat, utilizing my budding ukulele skills and my love for teaching.

About fifteen minutes after the email went out, I got the first notification that I had someone signed up. When I checked, it was not one of the ones who had told me they were interested. I was ecstatic! This meant with the few individuals who had already told me they wanted to learn, we would have five or six students. That's a managable number, so that I had enough time and focus to engage with each one individually. I got on the internet and began to make arrangements for the beginner ukuleles I would order and get set up for the students to buy when the next notification came in. Another new student. I was still pretty excited, and when the next two notifications came in back-to-back, I assumed they would be some of those early committers. Nope, two new ones. These two students weren't even at the youth group meeting where we had discussed the class. While I was beginning to do some tense mental math to figure out how many students that would make, another two notifications came in. When the evening was done, I had twenty emails expressing interest in the class. My first big idea here was blowing up, and I was terrified.

The prospect of purchasing twenty new ukuleles, inspecting them, stretching the strings, and getting them to students was daunting to say the least. The idea of having twenty student strangers in a room together with a ukulele they don't know how to play yet was more than daunting; it was overwhelming. I had barely gotten settled in this position and I was launching something that weighed heavily on my preparation time. And this would be the first real connection with many of these students, so it needed to go well. For a day, I prayed over and over, asking God if this was what our ministry was called to do at this time. I prayed for the courage to call it all off if it wasn't, and the guidance to see it done right if it was. And, at a little before midnight, I clicked the "purchase" button on the website, shipping myself twenty ukuleles.

Now, if you were to travel through the Milwaukee suburb of Elm Grove and stop at the Methodist church there, you might encounter a strange concentration of ukulele players in attendance. The group thrived and grew over several years, splitting into middle school and high school groups of almost twenty students each at their peak. A parents and adult class was formed. The local senior center caught wind of it and asked that we teach local seniors how to play too. Youth-led ukulele music was a common fixture in worship, even during the traditional service. And for several years, there was an annual ukulele concert on the front lawn of the church where everyone performed, worshipped, and celebrated the gift of music and community. It was larger than I could have ever imagined, but I almost didn't begin because of the fear I felt of going too big too fast.

Size matters in so much as God is calling you to a specific task that will take on a specific shape. God calls us to small and large tasks alike, and neither is greater than the other. Jesus fed thousands and sat with one woman at the well in his ministry. The disciples converted thousands at Pentecost but also stopped to talk to a single Eunuch. In each case, the size of the endeavor was right for the moment and the call.

The point of all of these examples is to broaden your perception, because if you only listen for large calls, you miss invitations to small miracles. If you only listen for God calling you to do what you've always done, you miss God calling you to the new hearts being changed in your midst. To properly discern your call, to truly listen and experience what God has for you and your church, you must come with no preconceived notions.

For the great doesn't happen through impulse alone, and is a succession of little things that are brought together.

—Vincent van Gogh, *Vincent van Gogh: The Complete Letters*

Chapter 10
Best Practices

Not all new faith expressions are new to the world, perhaps only new to your church. That's good news because it means that other people are actively working through the practical execution within the space.

Entirely new or unique expressions are rare. It would be unusual to find your church called to do something no one else in the ministry world is doing. So, knowing that there is (often) nothing new under the sun, we have an opportunity to give ourselves the best chances for success by researching other people and churches. When discernment leads to a new expression or ministry, a smart first step is to reach out to every pastor and ministry leader you know and ask, "Who else is doing this?" and if there are enough, asking the follow-up, "Who's doing this WELL?" This will help you determine some best practices. Some of the most valuable planning you can do for your new expression is to find someone else who is doing it well and learning from their process, mistakes, and successes.

What worked well? How would you do it even better?

What flopped? Why did it flop?

What was something you wish you knew before you began?

How was the event different the second time you did it?

What problems have you had and solved so far?

It is one thing to learn from your own mistakes through a rocky first meeting or event, but it's a completely different and more helpful thing to learn from the mistakes of another ministry that has been failing, learning, and adapting through their own development of their expression. While plenty of what other churches will experience is going to be specific to their context, there will also be plenty of lessons to learn and apply. There is no such thing as too much information when you are working to plan something completely new to you. It's like being able to look into the future and predict the unforeseen issues ahead of time so you can prepare for them.

Too often our events or expressions fail because of the same mistakes others have made before us. Finding a clergy forum or asking your ministry leader networks for their experiences regarding what you are looking to execute is the best way to anticipate the issues you will face and will often be more thorough than the most insightful, creative, experienced planner. Ask the questions rather than finding out the hard way.

Sometimes we vainly consider ourselves to be that "most insightful, creative, experienced" planner or leader. This is a dangerous place to live in ministry, especially if you are right. You might, after years of hard work and achievement, gain a reputation as an innovative, creative, effective leader. You might be passionate, a risk-taker who supports new ideas and leads with an ethos of "Yes, let's try that!" But when you are humble enough to ask the question, "Who else is doing this too?" and honestly to listen and reflect on their input, your ministry will improve. And you'll find yourself connecting with new people who are also creative and innovative, who have completely different experiences and views. Through their eyes and thoughts, you'll see the gaping holes in your ability and understanding. We can interpret Proverbs 1:5, "let the wise listen and add to their learning, and let the discerning get guidance—" as a personal invitation to accept the guidance of others in our own discernment. With the help of others, we can be better than we ever could on our own, and with disciplined humility we can ask, listen, reflect, and trust.

Team Sport

When you go into the world to begin the search for best practices, don't be afraid to collaborate with anyone and everyone who might have a productive insight. There are a few qualifiers in that statement, so I want to expand on it. Building the kingdom of God is a team sport. We work together toward a common goal outside of our own church, our region, our denomination, and even our belief structures. Being willing to converse with and learn from a church that is in a different tradition or holds to a different theology can still be incredibly useful to your event. We are not competing with other Christian traditions or expressions; we are all tasked by Jesus to make disciples. That is, anyone and everyone. Good information is good information and can lead to a more fruitful event or lay the groundwork for your new ministry. But the other side of that coin is that you do not have to entertain insight that is not productive. Sometimes the "anyone and everyone" wants to share thoughts, opinions, or objections to your discerned expression. While they are entitled to those thoughts and opinions, you certainly do not have to entertain their objections as insight unless they are practical objections.

For example, imagine you have discerned a call to a new faith expression like a large-scale raffle like Cow Pie Bingo and, in your search for best practices, a church or ministry leader shares a warning that you have to have a raffle license to do such an event and that in their opinion, the paperwork is not worth the hassle or profit. They may even frame their reflections negatively, calling the idea "stupid." That is their opinion, and though framed negatively and less constructively, the statement may warrant a follow-up question about the details that led to that opinion. How much did they make? What was the "hassle" mentioned? Did they use the raffle license for other things after this event? If they were forced to do it again, what would they do differently? Round out their response to better understand their opinion, because it is an opinion about the practical side of the event and was created using context-specific events and factors.

If instead the church or ministry leader accosts you for violating their interpretation of "Then He said to me, "See, I will give you cow's dung in place of human dung over which you will prepare your bread" (Ezekiel 4:15 NASB) and not using the cow's dung to bake bread to eat, then you should pass that input by. Theological differences with others are not deciding factors in your own discernment, and at this stage they are unhelpful unless they lend practical insight to the expression of that discernment.

Also, that would be super gross.

Unfortunately, there are plenty of Christian leaders and churches that will not see past the theological divides to provide any sort of help. Some will openly disagree with the new expression itself, your leadership, your church's legitimacy, and the call you have discerned. These moments are one of scriptural reflection, namely Matthew 10:14. Shake the dust off your feet and move on. The churches that are moving and experiencing their call in new and exciting ways are the ones that understand the ecumenical and collaborative strength we are capable of and the role it will play in any form of revival in the coming decades. These are the churches and leaders you should align yourself with and learn from. The rest are just dusty.

Pay It Forward

As a response to a new expression or a healthy current expression, be willing to help when others are in need of best practices too. If those outside your own tradition are poking and prodding your ministry or you as a leader, it is easy to become closeminded. But if we trust that God is speaking in our midst, and that others can hear and discern, we should be willing to help nurture the call of others. Ministry spaces should be ecumenical sounding boards and think tanks, not clandestine affairs. We do not have proprietary claim to what God has called us to do. Building the kingdom of God is not about keeping our blueprints hidden away. Instead, just as you would give yourself the best chance of success in your call, be willing to share constructive feedback with those who ask.

There is a narrow center of this spectrum that is fruitful, so be mindful. Keeping our successes and insights to ourselves is selfish and warped. But the other end of the spectrum is just as fruitless. Clergy gatherings and trainings can quickly devolve into long sessions of "Look how I already know this thing because of what my church does" instead of learning, listening, growing. Bravado in ministry is often covering an unwillingness to risk growing into new space or to try a new thing. Boasting of our own ministerial prowess or ingenuity is not helpful to others, and it does nothing to advance the kingdom of God. Instead, we should be listening to learn, with a willingness to share when we have meaningful input for others who may be looking to execute a similar call in their own context.

When other Ruby's Pantry sites came to see how we had rapidly become the largest site in the state, it was our duty of building the kingdom to help them facilitate feeding more people in any way we could. We showed them what we were doing and took the extra time to explain how we came to do it that way, often illustrating the failings that led to those decisions. While it would have been easy to keep our strategies and successes a secret, we didn't. It would have been equally easy to pretend we did everything right from the beginning and we're obviously very smart, but we didn't do that either. Instead, we became practiced at being completely open about our past shortcomings as they shaped our current successes so that our processes could be interpreted and reproduced in other contexts. It's humble work, but we are called to such humility as Christians. The parts that failed in the earliest Ruby's Pantry events were our fault as the people executing the mission of God, and we own it and grow from it. Sharing it with others for them to learn from is the best way to capitalize on our own failings to bring additional glory to God.

Seeking the best practices is what takes an untested idea, even if it's a well-planned untested idea, and gives it the best chances for success. If you are called by God to do something new in your church or ministry, give it the best chance for success, because too many times our calls fall flat because of our own missteps, our inability to find value in the input of others, or our unwillingness to ask for help. The body of the church is diverse and many faceted, so take advantage of the wealth of experience and knowledge out there to achieve what God has tasked you with.

Ask the questions, be humble, listen deeply, and learn from others.

A single conversation across the table with a wise man is better than ten years mere study of books.

—Henry Wadsworth Longfellow, *Hyperion*

Chapter 11

Stop Striving for Butts in the Pews

One of the more interesting things I learned about Bar+Church from Pastor Trevor Vaughn was that he never once invited someone who came to this new faith expression back to the church he was serving. Though this ministry was something that he was passionate about, the church he served was also something he was passionate about; and even though the concepts of faith communities and communal worship were things he was passionate about, there was never a time when he sought to bring individuals from Bar+Church into his congregation. Why? Because the church he served wasn't ready yet to be a part of the deep healing that needed to happen with these specific individuals.

Bar+Church served people who were at home in the bar and on edge in the pew. Whether explicitly or implicitly, they were made to feel unwelcomed in the sacred spaces that many congregations meet. For many of them, this severing from church and church culture meant severing ties with Jesus, whether they actively doubted or just put their faith in a box, closed it, and tucked it away. When Bar+Church became a space that they felt both safe and welcomed to discuss the hurts they were feeling, they began to heal and to understand Jesus among them right there in the bar in a way that simply could not happen in a church sanctuary. Why? Because they would never have put themselves in that space to let it. Amidst the alcohol and colorful language, people dressed for Saturday night out instead of Sunday best, God was moving and the kingdom was being rebuilt in the lives of these individuals. It didn't lead to bumps in Pastor Trevor's local church attendance, but it did bring a whole new group of people into a repaired relationship with Jesus.

Sometimes we look toward new faith expressions as opportunities to bring in more people to the church. Launch a new service, a new Bible study that meets in the trendy coffee shop, or an outreach that meets in a bar and we will finally bring in the stragglers. This alone is not a bad motive—to increase followers in a faith community, to build relationship and accountability in discipleship, and to worship together. These are cornerstones in church function. But when it becomes more about attendance records or budget dollars, we have a problem. Discerning our calling is about following God, not promoting our local church. We are called to the kingdom first. New faith expressions need to be more than getting butts in pews or—more likely—dollars in plates. Even in our current climate of financial shortfalls and the fear of closing churches, we are called to share the abundance of the kingdom with the world. That is a message that many churches and modern churchgoers need in these uncertain times, the hope that even now the kingdom of God is a kingdom of abundance. Unfortunately, the decline in most mainline denominations and the church as whole in the United States has us more worried about keeping our doors open than bringing the gospel to people.

We can't share the abundance of the kingdom of God through an attitude of scarcity.

Self-preservation is not evangelism; we're called to make disciples, not donors. We are called to build the kingdom of God, not the biggest church in town. If we do end up as the biggest church in town or have an influx of donors, it should be a by-product, a consequence of the real objective, which is bringing the gospel to new people. Starting something new isn't an avenue for bringing in budget dollars; it's an avenue for meeting new people where they are and creating faithful community. Faithful evangelism trusts in the provision of God; it doesn't fear the bottom line of the budget.

Consider new faith expressions as ways of laying foundation for a kingdom in which the church grows and thrives eventually, but that the church's survival and relevance is a consequence of the expression, not the primary goal. We don't start or maintain a youth ministry to bring giving dollars into the mix or to pad the worship numbers. We do it to help develop young, passionate disciples who will go and impact the world in ways that we never could imagine. We don't develop a Divorce Care Group to bring in one hundred new worshippers; we do it to share the supportive love of Christ with people who are in a vulnerable time of life. We aren't called to get more butts in pews; we're called to get more hearts into the kingdom. So, we meet people where they are, not worrying whether that place is the local church. It is possible that this new expression will bring people into a long-term trajectory toward church membership, but it may not be at our church, and it may not be with us. Meeting people where they are right now does not necessarily mean we are the people or church that will carry them into the next phase of their discipleship or faith development.

And that is okay.

As much as we may have been conditioned by the splitting, denomination-creating, and ecumenical infighting, bringing someone new into a relationship with Jesus that ends with them attending a different church is still a good thing. We are only part of any one person's faith journey for a time. There is no referral bonus at your church.

Meeting people where they are is not contingent on our ability to take them where they ultimately need to be. Their paths will ultimately weave through the world in complicated and unforeseen ways. Meeting people where they are is about beginning to form a relationship and learning to see Jesus in one another. For Bar+Church, it is the beginning of healing for the broken in a safe and familiar space. Perhaps someday they will move to a place of spiritual health and attend a local church. Hopefully, they will continue developing a heart for mission, the homeless, food insecurity, and their local community. It's even possible they may turn from a career as a construction worker to a career as a pastor like Trevor. But none of these things are day-one things, or the primary reason to start this process, or the mark of success of a new faith. Even these profound outcomes are not the mark of success for Bar+Church.

Meeting people where they are to help them for even a single moment on their journey from unbelief to belief, from frustration with God to falling even deeper in love with Christ—that is what this particular expression is all about, and there is a deep lesson to learn from it. The measure of success is the stories.

Stories of people feeding their neighbors and making new
friends;
Stories of drinking buddies in tears together praying;
Stories of bartenders debating theological points with pastors;
Stories of new believers at the bar wanting to take communion;
Stories of hearts changed by putting in the time.

For Farm Church, it's about working to feed people physically as much as spiritually in a space of food deserts and wide-
spread hunger. Hopefully the participants will go on to invite
more people, to use the mission to bring their neighbors into
a more secure space and lead them into discipleship. Perhaps it
may lead to new ministries and outreaches, helping those who
are dealing with hunger with money management, helping break
generational cycles of poverty, impacting an entire generation of
children who would have otherwise grown up in the systematic
oppression of the lower class and were doomed to continue a life
of scarcity. It could lead to dozens of new young families joining
the church who give generously and faithfully, because they have
experienced the fruits of this expression's labor and it changed
their lives. But for today, it's about feeding those who are hungry.
It's about loving neighbors in a way that sustains life. It may not
currently be bringing in giving dollars and helping to pad the
bottom line of the budget, but that is not what this particular
expression is all about. This expression, too, is measured in stories
of lives changed.

Stories of young people learning to turn soil and grow something good;

79

Stories of lonely people coming to connect over the task of
pulling weeds;
Stories of hungry children being fed fresh, organic food;
Stories of lost people being found by loving, caring farmers;
Stories of hearts healed by putting in the time.

For Ruby's Pantry in Jefferson, Wisconsin, it's about laypeople hearing the call of God and faithfully following to touch the lives of thousands of individuals and fill their cupboards. The volunteers for that site don't all attend the church. In fact, most do not. But once a month, they come together to be the hands and feet of Christ, making an impact that is felt across the state. It's possible it will lead to connections between the Christians volunteering and the others, sparking conversations about mission or gospel. It has already led to the development of other ministries and outreaches that branch out into different spaces to share the food brought to the community. Perhaps it will lead to those who receive their food share to contemplate the church and why it cares for them. I can tell you with certainty that even though the ministry brings in hundreds of volunteers and affects tens of thousands of lives, the church attendance has not gone up a single person directly because of it. It is still a success because it's also measured in stories.

Stories of Christians and non-Christians alike feeding the
hungry;
Stories of the working poor finally catching a break;
Stories of teenage volunteers learning about service;
Stories of food pantries and ministries springing up like
dandelions;
Stories of laypeople dreaming big dreams.

The largest religious demographic in our midst is "unchurched." We must make sure our motives are pure so that we can truly seek God's voice in our discernment. There are plenty of things to consider as part of the discernment process, like the mission and vision of the church and whether or not the church has the resources to accomplish what they believe they are being called to do. But if we are worried about money or numbers, we aren't listening for what God is telling us. Instead, follow God and build something good, something pure. Build something that is measured in the stories of its impact on real people.

Whether or not the butts come, the kingdom will.

Stories are data with a soul . . .

—Brené Brown

Chapter 12
Let's Get Weird

During the COVID-19 shutdown, the church I serve, perhaps like yours, had to figure out how to worship online effectively, which meant a culture shift in the congregation as well as a functional restructuring of the sanctuary. The leadership had to learn to plan and execute online worship, and the wider community had to become familiar with accessing the worship service broadcast over what was, for many of them, a new technology. The church adapted quickly and became able to worship from the comfort and safety of their homes and with the flexibility to worship wherever they found themselves on Sunday morning. Those traveling could be part of the community too. For over a year, the community learned and became comfortable with worshipping in this way together.

After the shutdown, this comfort and familiarity for these innovations within the church gave an interesting alternative to in-person worship in the right circumstances. For example, Christmas Day was on a Sunday in 2022, which meant for many churches a discussion surrounding attendance and volunteers' holiday plans; possible alternatives occurred when figuring out what Sunday/Christmas morning would look like. In years past when similar situations arose, one previous pastor planned a carol-singing event, so there would be minimal volunteers and he didn't have to write another sermon. Another pastor had a reading of a Christmas book for children, encouraging families to come in pajamas. A third pastor cancelled the service entirely, since the previous two solutions had mediocre attendances on top of the overall inconvenience for those who did choose to show up.

In all three situations, the decision was weighed: Sunday morning tradition against the increasingly diminishing likelihood that families would adjust their own family traditions to leave the house and physically visit the church. This was also a significant part of the conversation surrounding my own Advent planning in 2022.

The church being equipped for online worship was the first piece of the puzzle. It opened the door to new solutions not possible in the past. We could potentially pre-tape a service and broadcast it that Sunday morning. The congregation's familiarity with online worship because of the pandemic was another piece, knowing that the previous Advent, the church had done online worship exclusively and the congregation was both able and comfortable doing that. If the congregation would be comfortable with online worship exclusively on that Sunday, the church could reach the people who would have originally come in person on that particularly under-attended Sunday as well as those who would be willing to watch from home without having to interrupt their Christmas traditions. When these pieces were brought together and the worship team was on board, the opportunity took shape to do something unique with this service, since we were not constrained by having to execute the service live. If we weren't simply providing a live-stream of what was occurring in real time in the sanctuary, we could break out of that box and begin to think about new and different ways to worship through video streaming. This is where my own discernment brought forth a new idea, and things got weird.

Through my prayer time and discernment practices, the word comfort kept rising to the surface. People would be gathered in their homes and with their families, surrounded by the warmth and comfort of tradition. They might even be in comfy pajamas, cozied up together under a blanket with a cup of coffee. This is how people would be watching the worship service together, and I wanted to connect with the overwhelming sense of comfort and togetherness. To start, I asked others what nostalgia surrounded their Christmas seasons: What sources of comfort did they find in the familiar rhythms of Christmas? What did Christmas morning look like? What could you count on each year that brought your family together? My wife shared with me the memory of her family watching an animated Christmas special each year that was absurd, silly, and connected her to a time in which her distant and busy siblings were just carefree kids, celebrating together as a family. It stirred in me memories of watching the one Claymation special my family had on VHS when I was growing up and that same excitement to watch it together each year.

With this, the idea was planted. What if we did an animated special as a worship expression for Christmas morning? I mean, is that even something we could do? I looked at how the animated special my wife loves was formatted, somewhere between a variety show and a service of homilies and hymns, and began researching how to do (very) basic animation. It was a difficult undertaking and was more work than an average service, but the way that the service connected with people was nothing short of miraculous. People were connected to memories of animated specials, celebrated the birth of Jesus in a new way, and watched in the comfort of their own homes with their extended families; and the video had a viewership of twenty times any other worship this church had ever put online. To put it in terms of previous chapters, I began hearing stories of people who somehow found the animated video on Facebook and it led them to our YouTube site where all of my sermons are displayed.

We took the opportunity to use technology new to us to meet new people where they were. And truly, the technology wasn't even that new—we were emulating animated specials from the 1980s. But the callback and novelty of it brought people into a space to see just what it was all about. It meant unchurched people scrolling through Facebook or YouTube paused for a moment and heard songs and scriptures about the birth of Jesus. In the following week, every sermon video on our YouTube channel received a viewer bump. We got weird, and it connected with new people in a new way.

This is not a new idea. This book has talked about new faith expressions and new-to-you faith expressions in a way that would make it easy to forget that our entire history is steeped in breaking norms to reach new people. John Wesley saw a growing divide and took the church outdoors to people who were not, shall we say, avid churchgoers. He went to the coal mines and prisons in the late 1700s, preaching in a way that called back to Jesus on the shoreline in chapter one. John Wesley and Jesus got weird with how they brought the message to people and amazing things happened.

In Wesley's time, these field preaching practices were described by Wesley's contemporaries as vile. In his journal, Wesley wrote that he "submitted to be more vile" as he continued to reach out in these spaces and in these ways to share the gospel, and in doing so connected with thousands of new believers. Eventually, his words would reach astronomical numbers of people, and would found a movement that would stretch to every corner of the world. He followed his call to a new place through a new faith expression, which was an expression of Jesus preaching and teaching in the midst of the ceremonial unclean over a thousand years before. You could call that story of the sermon on the beach at the Lake of Gennesaret Jesus "submitting to be more vile." Pivotal moments in church history are found in moments where great Christians have found themselves submitting to be more vile to share the gospel. This, in a nutshell, is what the modern church needs to embrace in their discernment of where to go from here—a willingness to change tactics from the traditional to the previously unthinkable. The church needs to be open to wherever God may send us, whether it be the beaches or the fields. Or, to put it as perfectly as Methodist Fresh Expressions expert Michael Beck did in his Fresh Expressions article with the same title, "Make Methodism Vile Again."

Discernment of God's call for your church or ministry needs to be done with an attitude of openness to the previously vile, the weird, and the absurd. This is how the church is going to be able to present to new people in new contexts, with new ideas that utilize new medias and new constraints. Learning to animate for this worship service was absolutely absurd, but the outcome was nothing short of miraculous. Our Christmas animation took our worship service into over twelve hundred homes. It met people where they were in a new way and brought an opportunity to connect. It brought songs and stories of the gospel to more people than any one worship service within our church walls ever has.

An openness to embracing the strange, unique, or new is what leads people to drop everything and start a church on a farm.

It leads to people thinking differently about haircuts. It inspires people to try bold things in the shadow of a pandemic. It connects people through new technologies. It brings the gospel message into unlikely places. In short, it builds the kingdom of God, and it does so with all the tools we have at our disposal.

Fresh expressions are popping up in cafes, movie theaters, bars, tattoo parlors, and in biker clubs. A ministry I've consulted with is supporting and evangelizing to performers in strip clubs. Churches are just scratching the surface of what can be done on social media apps like Instagram or TikTok. We live in a new reality that is driven by both content creation and technology to share that content with the world, readily available and easily accessed. In your pocket right now is a computer with a camera that is able to take video testimonials, edit them, and post them on the church's social media. That phone is also capable of taking silly videos of your church worship team doing a dance and putting that dance in spaces that convey the spirit of fun and joy your church has to your community and the world. It has the ability to broadcast live from spaces of worship or revival, for the community to be a part of the Holy Spirit moving. Technology has transformed communication to a space of accessibility that was previously unimaginable. The only limit is the imagination of the church and its willingness to follow God into previously uncharted and occasionally taboo spaces.

A huge difficulty surrounding new faith expressions that are particularly unique is limited willingness—the reluctance of the church or ministry community to embrace the "new." It can be difficult to think openly about things a church has never done before or do things in a completely different way. It can even seem like the way we've always done something is the only Christian way to do it. In some cases, the "new" is approached with an attitude of worldliness that Christians actively work to avoid in most contexts.

"Why should the church be on the same media app that has other content providers using inappropriate language or engaging in adult themes? Jesus built a church without TikTok!"

"Why should the church be dabbling in things that other churches aren't doing? Obviously these things are undignified for churches to do. Otherwise, everyone would be doing it!"

"People should get on board with what the church has always done. It's worked before, and it will work again without all of these bells and whistles."

These objections to innovation can block what God is specifically calling you and your ministry to do within your context. Entering into new contexts should be met with excitement, optimism, and careful execution. Instead, it's often met with dread, pessimism, and avoidance. God is calling us into all sorts of spaces, especially those untapped corners of the world. You can even consider these avenues as new mission fields. God is calling ministries and churches onto new social media platforms, to utilize new opportunities within the community, and to do things no church has ever done before. It's not always easy though. As Margaret Wheatley wrote in her book *Leadership and the New Science*, "It's scary work, trying to find a new world, hoping we won't die in the process."[1] That is many congregants' fear—that the church will

1. Margaret Wheatley, *Leadership and the New Science*, 2nd ed. (Berrett-Koehler, 1999), 173–74.

lose itself or become something it's not by changing. But change is what drives the church to fulfill its creation, and it always has. It's exciting and scary, but if the discernment is solid, the weird should be just as accessible as the familiar. If the church is going to make disciples of all nations, it must realize that the calls will lead to new spaces or to utilize new ways of accessing familiar spaces. If the church wants to reach people it has never reached before, it must be willing to do what no church is doing.

Remember, the largest religious demographic in your community is unchurched people, so there are so many people not being reached by the churches in your context. To reach them, we need to be willing to follow wherever and however God is calling us. So if God makes the call, we must be willing to go to the weird places too.

To be faithful in discernment, we need to be willing to take on the strange opportunities God puts before us. Encourage your laity to think outside the box to see where God might be pointing. Get weird, because there are people living in the weird places in the world that need to hear the gospel, too, and God is already there working and calling you to join in. People are weird, unique, outrageous, and absurd; our church and ministries must be willing to be, too.

A pastor friend I know plays Call of Duty every night online with a group of other pastor friends. In their gaming, there isn't shop talk about churches, ministry, or theology. Mainly there's playful banter around the game itself, full of jokes and jabs about one another's abilities. One night, the pastor and his friends played a round with a stranger who was a good player and fun to have on the chat, so they invited him to continue playing with them and he became a semi-regular participant. No ministry or theology, just nice people playing a video game each night on the internet and building relationships together. Eventually this stranger became a friend, sharing his life situation and issues, and this group was there to provide comfort and distraction as the man went through a failed marriage, a loss of housing, and eventually getting back on his feet and remarried. Through all of it, my pastor friend was there and connected, doing ministry in this new, unlikely way: while playing video games online. The end of that story is that my friend officiated the wedding of the man and his new wife, meeting this online friend in person across the country. But the story of what this might mean in my friend's ministry and his call was just beginning. He is actively in discernment with God and his faith community to find out if God is calling a broader group into this unique ministry opportunity. He's actively praying whether or not God is calling his church to an online Call of Duty ministry, and it's weird.

It's weird and it's outside what that church community has ever done, and it has the potential to reach people who otherwise would never hear the love of Jesus Christ through the love of neighbor, through relationship and community.

Ask God for a direction, find where the people are, and follow God toward that space. God is actively working in every community. The only limitation on the church's involvement in those spaces is how much the church is willing to engage. Discernment should live in spaces that welcome creativity, hope, and unapologetic departures from the norm. Where is God working and calling out to your ministry to join? Is it weird? I hope so, because God is in those places meeting brand-new people and paving the way for faithful servants to build community, relationships, and the kingdom of God.

To faithfully discern God's call, you must be willing to hear it wherever it might lead you. And if it's calling you, your church, or your new expression out to the coal mines, the work camps, or somewhere especially vile, be ready.

Renewal will not come from imitating the past. It will not come from a nostalgic longing for the empire days of a culture gone or going, nor from adopting values alien to God's revelation in Christ.

—Lovett H. Weems, Jr., *Church Leadership: The Practice of Ministry*

Chapter 13

Do It, Already

In 2017, I was serving at a larger church in the suburbs of Milwaukee. Other than a pair of nondenominational behemoth churches, my church was one of the few that could afford a youth leader on staff, let alone a hefty youth budget and facility. I was working with a group of other local youth leaders from a half dozen churches to plan an ecumenical youth retreat. The hope was that this retreat could facilitate smaller churches with less funding to experience a larger-scale event with all the bells and whistles a larger congregation and ministry might afford. As a leader with a generous budget that could spearhead that project, I had discerned God's call to help other churches to participate in the types of spiritual retreat, discipleship, and worship we were able to execute in our congregation. I connected with a few other youth leaders with resources to see this event into existence, gathering my team. One leader had a talented praise band at their church, another had years of experience at the youth camp facility we were look-ing to rent, and a third had experience working with several of the smaller churches in our region doing ecumenical worship services around Ash Wednesday and Good Friday in the past.

We recruited several church leaders and volunteers from other churches to help understand the landscape of the different local communities represented with the dozens of churches that voiced an interest in being part of the retreat. We even trusted God and the vision and our discernment when we began getting pushback from some churches not wanting to work with us, and our own churches questioning why we should use our funds to provide for other churches. None of it could dampen our spirits. God was in this mission, we knew it. So we forged ahead, being mindful of every detail we could consider to make this event a success. There were weekly meetings to discuss ideas, to plan and replan each game and activity, to design journals and T-shirts, to pick worship sets for the band, and to outline messages for me to lead the group in during our sessions.

We crossed all the *T*s and dotted every single *I*.

We met.

And met.

. . . and met.

. . . and met some more.

Before long, our fall retreat had to be pushed to be a spring retreat. The praise band's leader took a new job in a different community and wasn't available anymore to work with the band, which eventually fell apart. Our worship plan had to be reworked and our budget adjusted to hire a group to come in and lead music. The new dates that worked best for our large ecumenical retreat wouldn't work because of the facility's existing camps, so we had to coordinate over and over with dozens of youth leaders to try to accommodate everyone. The roll over to a new calendar year brought a significant drop in a collaborating church's budget, causing the costs for participating churches and members to rise. A few churches dropped out, because it was beginning to look like this event was never going to happen.

How could this be? Did we misunderstand God's call into this retreat?

Hadn't we listened? Discerned together? Gathered a team?

Was this all some big mistake?

That seemed impossible with the amount of visioning and prayer involved with the planning we had done. Again and again, at every level of planning we stepped back and asked if we were still remaining true to the vision on our hearts and the call of God for our ministries. What had felt so life-giving at the beginning began to feel like a grind, filled with frustration and doubt. When the event date finally came, the churches involved enjoyed worshipping together, learning and growing, and leaving with hope of a future event. One of the participating church leaders commented as they packed up their bus, "We weren't sure this was going to happen. I'm glad y'all finally decided to figure it out!"

What we eventually learned in this process was that faithful discernment is a powerful thing, and should lead to thorough planning, but discernment and planning must lead to execution. Otherwise, we are wasting our calls on an elaborate thought experiment, and in the case of this retreat, the time and resources of other ministries.

Too Many Cooks, Not Enough Tasters

One issue we identified looking back was that we had built a team to lead, which was important, but then we kept expanding that team to get greater buy-in with the many ministries involved from a diverse group of denominations. In doing so, we had created a "Create-by-Committee" culture, which moves at a snail's pace and is often ineffective. Suddenly even the most minor detail took days to decide, after a series of emails or phone calls. We had focused on diverse voices and creative buy-in at the cost of functionality of planning. There were plenty of ways of connecting and elevating voices from different denominations and traditions without having each leader in on each decision. We had tried to do too much with too many, and ended up with very little.

When churches started backing out of the retreat, we decided it was necessary to move back to the original team of four leaders, connected through the vision and call they shared for this event. We found ways of using the other leaders for the event itself, and we also found that many of the leaders were relieved to not be expected to help at all. They simply wanted to experience the retreat with their students. These leaders didn't share the call or vision to create this event; they just saw it as a great opportunity for their own students and church budgets, and that was fine. Actually, that's great! They valued what we were doing and were excited to participate. They weren't interested in cooking the meal; they were wanting to consume it and enjoy it, which was the whole reason we were putting on the event in the first place.

Following God's call to a new faith expression is only following if it comes to fruition. An event planned but not executed does not build the kingdom of God, or engage young believers in powerful worship, or promote a unified spirit among believers within the community. It isn't the amazing or miraculous thing God has been inviting you to be a part of. Mostly it's just a waste of time and passion.

Divine Safety Net

The event ended up working out, with about two-thirds of the original groups in attendance. The hundreds of teens in attendance were able to be a part of something profound only because we didn't give up. In the few years we did this retreat we tried new themes that were uninspiring, activities that flopped, and mistakenly scheduled one retreat on the same weekend as homecoming for several of the churches' youth. When we met to review after an event, we never had to search far to find ways that we could've done better with the task God set forth. And through it all, each event brought in more youth than the previous (except during that homecoming weekend!) and churches kept coming back. New youth leaders emerged and nurtured their own calls in their faith. New relationships and friendships were born. God was the safety net in which we were able to still do amazing things even when we fell short. The model was replicated three more times before all the original leadership had moved on to other churches or out of ministry, and the event was over. But hearts had been moved, and a small corner of the kingdom was built for the future generation of disciples. God was present in the event God called us to provide, as promised.

When I was fourteen years old, my dad took my younger sister and I indoor rock climbing at our local wellness center. We trained in tying the knots and using the harnesses, and finally we got to do the climbing. I was excited to climb next to my sister, who was only eleven years old and a lot less athletic than I was at the time, because, if you have a younger sibling you know, we of course had to race to the top. We looked over at each other and it was on. I started climbing, fingers in the grooved holds, lifting one leg, then the other. Up, over, over, back, up I went, focusing solely on the next move. I completely ignored the fatigue in my hands until the shaking got so bad my hands simply locked up. I was so tired and sore, holding on for dear life. My hands were clenching so hard, I could barely feel them and I was stuck.

A little panicked, I looked over at my sister, suddenly worried she, too, was struggling. But no, she wasn't struggling. In fact, at that very moment, she was about five feet higher than I was, no hands on the wall, leaning back into her harness looking down at me. I was climbing as if I had no safety system, relying on my feeble hand strength and five minutes of experience. My sister was fully relaxed and took periodic breaks on her climb to the top, resting back in her safety harness. When she reached the top, she even jumped backward off the wall, letting the ropes catch her and gently lower her down.

Trust your support structure. It changes things. If you've discerned a call for yourself or your ministry, and God has your back as spiritual safety net, all of a sudden trusting God becomes so much easier. Bias toward action and execution becomes inevitable. Don't be too afraid of messing up that there's no forward momentum. Don't let the unknown stall you in executing the expression you have been called to build. If God's got your back, throw a little caution to the wind and trust that doing it with God's help is better than sitting around waiting until you feel like the plan is perfect.

The best time to plant a tree was 20 years ago.
The second-best time is now

—Chinese proverb

Chapter 14
All Together Now

It can seem like it's never the right time to start something new or go out on a limb, regardless of how loudly God may be calling you. The church volunteers are already overworked, the budget is already spent, or the people who give the most won't like it. But it's always the right time to pursue what God has ordained in us. Our call should put us in uncomfortable spaces, but it never does so alone or without a plan. Many of the personal examples and stories I've shared with you as examples of new faith expressions happened in the midst of a decades-long downward spiral in church vitality. Farm Church, Bar+Church, school haircuts, and donated undies were all endeavors discerned by leaders and churches that could see that the way things were going wasn't cutting it. They are just a few examples of many faithful people trying new things to connect with new people through their own calls. These examples can bring hope and inspiration.

But for every church or ministry that is willing to try something new or weird, there were plenty that are set in their ways. They have been operating the same way for as long as anyone can remember, so why change anything now? The world around our churches has changed, and that is sometimes viewed as a problem to overcome, not an invitation.

In early 2020, churches across America were mandated to stop congregating in person. It felt like overnight, churches had to change. We had to find new ways to connect as a community when physical closeness was prohibited. Pastors and church leaders were scrambling to learn all they could about streaming over the internet, cameras and lighting, and virtual conferencing. It was a terrifying time and experience for many, and not all churches weathered the experience. Perhaps in your own community there is a new bank or daycare facility that has some impressive stained-glass windows. You may have noticed that there are a lot of pews for sale on Facebook Marketplace.

Even now, with the surviving churches reopened and returning to what they did prior to the COVID-19 shutdown, there are lasting scars that will likely never heal. After this forced season of innovation, the attitude for many churches toward change and growth stayed the same, and many abandoned all of the creativity and spirit of flexibility they had learned. Why? Because many of the issues plaguing churches post-COVID were present and plaguing the same churches pre-COVID. The forward momentum in many denominations and local congregations has been waning for decades. We've been in a spiral of managed decline as culture has barreled forward into new spaces, new technologies, new challenges, and new opportunities. And, as the drop-off grows more and more severe, we must admit that we've mismanaged the decline.

As Bishop Dottie Escobedo-Frank put it, "While the church has been hiding inside the walls for fear of death and decline, the world around has encountered remarkable growth and change."[1] The church has hunkered down in complacency while each gen-

---

1. Rudy Rasmus and Dottie Escobedo-Frank, *Jesus Insurgency: The Church Revolution from the Edge* (Abingdon Press, 2012), 4

eration has become less and less churched. It has become more commonplace to hear, "Well, we used to . . ." than "Let's try something new!"

"Remember when . . ." than "Imagine if . . .""We've never . . ." than "Why not?"

When we use the phrase *We used to . . .*, we are describing something that has finished. It ran its course and, in the best of cases, was fruitful and then gracefully finished. It was successful in the time it was executed, but it did not endure; it fit a context and a time we no longer exist within. The things that worked then didn't continue to work then, and likely will not work now because we are in a new time, a new place, and a new context. When we use the phrase *We've never . . .* , we are admitting that we no longer trust that God is in control. We forget how to dream and wonder at the possibilities that a boundless God could be calling us into. We settle back on what we've done before as the benchmark of what is possible for us in the future, instead of asking the bold question of *how*.

Used to, remember when, we've never—these are phrases of a church so inward and backward-focused that it's possible they don't even realize that the world has left them behind. In *Congregations in Transition: A Guide for Analyzing, Assessing, and Adapting in Changing Communities*, authors Nancy Ammerman and Carly S. Dudley wrote, "One of the first things we discovered about adapting congregations was that they simply notice what is going on around them. Declining congregations often barely realize that the world has changed."[2] Declining congregations haven't

---

2. Nancy Ammerman and Carly S. Dudley, *Congregations in Transition: A Guide for Analyzing, Assessing, and Adapting in Changing Communities* (Jossey-Bass, 2002), 8

kept up with the world because they're too busy looking at the things that are finished instead of what might be coming.

Times have changed. Culture has changed. Families have changed. Teenagers have changed. Life has changed. The church has not. The church has remained stationary.

Many of the church's ministries have remained the same, declined, and failed.

Many of our church and worship styles have remained and staled.

While the culture has grown and evolved, the church got stuck.

But God, too, has remained.

God has remained unchanged in God's faithful commitment to humanity.

And God has remained with God's people in every new place we explore.

While the church has become stagnant in its steadfastness, God has been steadfast in God's ongoing pursuit of humanity. God has continued amid these new cultures, new technologies, new challenges, and new opportunities. God has been relentless, even as the church has slowed and stopped in that pursuit to be present and engaging in these new spaces. This is so frustrating because there was a time when new expressions and innovations were embraced heartily by the church. When the church was growing and thriving, it was working to find Christ amidst new contexts and using new means. The Gutenberg printing press was invented in the 1450s. Its moveable face type and the press meant that books could now be printed in larger numbers, sold cheaply, and distributed widely.

Bibles began being printed almost immediately, making them accessible to the common person. Martin Luther's *95 Theses* was a pamphlet printed and widely distributed. The Reformation might not have been possible without the utilization of this new media. Radio was first widely commercially available in 1920, and in 1923 Calvary Baptist Church in New York began to operate its own radio station to evangelize. Television overtook radio as the most popular broadcast medium in the 1950s, and several radio preachers switched over immediately, including Archbishop Fulton Sheen, deemed the "first televangelist" by *TIME* in an issue in 1952. During this time, every corner of the globe saw the introduction of missionary efforts to bring the gospel. The church was using new tools and going to new contexts to share the gospel.

Since the very first Christians crossed the ocean to America, many churches and denominations have seen adaptions and new ways of thinking in their understanding of slavery, people of color in the clergy, and women serving churches as both ministry leaders and clergy. But somewhere along the line, the peak of the Christian movement found the top of the parabola. The church slowed in its pursuit of new evangelism tools, fresh ways to engage, and new communities to engage with. The motivation to seek God working in new ways faltered. As the church plateaued and eventually began to decline in the US, we became comfortable with the people in the pews next to us instead of focusing outward to reach the people we have missed. We became comfortable and complacent. And today many churches consider their best days behind them.

Still, God is calling them.

Wesley's field preaching is a blueprint for innovation, a part of our very DNA, not just an antiquated practice from the past.

The church is being called out of the past into something new, a reflection of Jesus's preaching on the shores of Gennesaret.

Pastor Ben Johnston-Krase shared these words at the NEXT Conference in 2016 when speaking about planting Farm Church: "We are managing decline. . . . We are managing decline and it's the most exciting time to be in ministry ever. Here's why—because we are managing decline not because our culture has left us behind, but rather because God has gone on ahead of us and God is doing stuff that we haven't figured out yet. So that's what we've got to tell ourselves—to keep up with Jesus, right? We don't need to bring people to God, we need to trust that God is already doing stuff. We do not need to bring people to Christ, we need to strive to see Christ in other people. And we don't need to just invoke the Holy Spirit, we need to trust the Holy Spirit is invoking us beyond a church we've ever known, beyond the church we were trained to serve, into a church that God is actively working to form."

God is not in decline; God is moving in the world as much as ever.

The church needs to catch up to what Jesus is doing already in our midst.

Jesus is where the people are. We need to go to the people. We need to listen to where God is calling us because that is where Jesus has been working all this time.

Clear away the preconceived notions of what God might want, the fear of the unknown, the anxiety of decline. Be still and listen. God is calling you, your congregation, me, and the entire church by name with an invitation to the miraculous.

This is the work of discernment; of listening to God and understanding the context; of preparing faithfully to execute and act upon the call; to empower the laity to hear their call and act; to faithfully follow where God is desperately calling the church to engage. Yes, we are in a multi-decade decline in church attendance. Yes, we are living in what is being described as a post-Christian world and have been for decades. The global pandemic in 2020 turned up the already-present need for churches to experience new life and new faith expressions, and God is calling.

Jesus told his disciples to go and make disciples of all nations, which is a tall order and it's only getting taller. The world has never needed Jesus more. Since the day Jesus spoke those words to today, the mandate has remained the same: to go and out and meet people where they are. All the people in all the places.

The church is in trouble, but God has never been anything but strong, faithful, and calling. God's help is readily available; that is part of the very nature of God. God's help and guidance are available if we simply ask and are willing to do the work to understand. We need to listen, to discern, to prepare, and to do. If we can do that, not only will we find new ways to build the kingdom of God but also we will change the hearts and lives of the people around us.

We will hear stories of how God has worked through us to create new things.

We will hear stories of how Jesus has brought hope to the broken.

We will hear stories of how the Spirit burns in the hearts of new believers.

We will hear stories of miracles happening in our communities.

We will hear stories of dead churches being brought back to life.

We will hear stories of a new church moving the world.

And it will be beyond a church we have ever known, a church that God is still building through us.

Go, and do.

Therefore go and make disciples of all nations, baptizing them
in the name of the Father and of the Son and of the Holy Spirit,
and teaching them to obey everything I have commanded you.
And surely I am with you always, to the very end of the age.

—Matthew 28:19-20 NIV

At abingdonpress.com/called-out-extras, you'll find The Point of Application, a resource for church leaders and ministry teams to use together. It follows the chapters of this book, providing questions and exercises to help you apply the ideas and principles you've read about here. Work through the Point of Application process together, and you'll see more clearly where God is calling your ministry to go. You may, of course, use the resource individually, too, but it is most powerful when used by ministry leaders and teams.